HOW BASKETBALL WORKS

Keltie Thomas

Illustrations by Greg Hall

MAPLE TREE PRESS

Maple Tree Press Inc.
51 Front Street East, Suite 200, Toronto, Ontario M5E 1B3
www.mapletreepress.com

Text © 2005 Keltie Thomas
Illustrations © 2005 Greg Hall

Distributed in Canada by Raincoast Books
9050 Shaughnessy Street, Vancouver, British Columbia V6P 6E5

Distributed in the United States by Publishers Group West
1700 Fourth Street, Berkeley, California 94710

We acknowledge the financial support of the Canada Council for the
Arts, the Ontario Arts Council, the Government of Canada through
the Book Publishing Industry Development Program (BPIDP), and the
Government of Ontario through the Ontario Media Development
Corporation's Book Initiative for our publishing activities.

ONTARIO ARTS COUNCIL
CONSEIL DES ARTS DE L'ONTARIO

Dedication
For my mom, whose high school teammates
called her a "tiger on the court"

Acknowledgments
A special thanks to all the fantastic people at Maple Tree Press, Greg
Hall, Jason Andrade, Basketball Ontario, Matt Zeysing, Naismith
Memorial Basketball Hall of Fame, Paul Bies, Bob Llewellyn, Tom
Shinn, Spalding, Taylor Bies, Kadeem Green, and, of course, P-J

Cataloguing in Publication Data
Thomas, Keltie
How basketball works / Keltie Thomas ; illustrations by Greg Hall.
(How sports work)
Includes index.
ISBN 1-897066-18-X (bound).—ISBN 1-897066-19-8 (pbk.)
1. Basketball—Juvenile literature. I. Hall, Greg, 1963– II. Title. III.
Series.
GV885.1.T48 2005   j796.323   C2004-905590-9

Design & art direction: Greg Hall ; Illustrations: Greg Hall
Photo credits: see page 64

Printed in Belgium

A B C D E F

Contents

4 **How Does Basketball Work?**
6 **Legends of the Game**
How Earth Became "Planet Hoops"

Chapter 1

7 **That's the Way the Ball Bounces**
14 **Legends of the Game**
Houdini of the Hardwood

Chapter 2

15 **Court of Action**
22 **Legends of the Game**
Saved in the Nick of Time

Chapter 3

23 **Game Wear**
30 **Legends of the Game**
Swooping in Feet First

Chapter 4

31 **The Complete Athlete**

38 **Legends of the Game**

When Michael Jordan Didn't Make the Cut

Chapter 5

39 **The Science of Explosive Moves**

46 **Legends of the Game**

Dr. J Operates on the Hoop

Chapter 6

47 **How Pros Measure Up**

52 **Legends of the Game**

As Good as Advertised?

Chapter 7

53 **Offense vs. Defense**

60 **Legends of the Game**

When Mr. Defense Met
the Ultimate Scoring Machine

61 **Rules and Regs**

62 **Basketball Talk**

64 **Index and Answers**

Fans, players, and inquiring minds everywhere want to know!

What makes basketball one of the most action-packed and high-scoring games on Earth? How did planet Earth get game? What makes the ball so bouncy? What's the first riddle of hoops? How can players get stiffed by the rim? How come so many basketball stars are so tall? How can you dribble like a pro? How do pros make opponents go mental? What pumps up basketball shoes to rock the court?

Well, just like everything else on Earth, it all comes down to science (plus a few things science hasn't managed to explain yet!). And if you think that makes basketball sound boring, you'd better check what planet you're on. But, hey, why don't you turn the page and check out the world of basketball in action for yourself. Whether you want answers to those burning questions, tips on becoming a better player, the scoop on inside information, or just to get in the game, this book's for you.

PSSSST. YOU DON'T HAVE TO BE A BASKETBALL FANATIC TO READ THIS BOOK. THE RULES AND REGS AND BASKETBALL TALK ARE DECODED ON PAGE 61.

James Naismith

How Earth Became "Planet Hoops"

Planet Earth had got no game before 1891. There was baseball, football, and soccer. But come winter, when the northern half of the planet froze, guys and gals had no indoor game to play without tearing up the gym and jarring their bones.

Many were bored, especially the guys at the YMCA in Springfield, Massachusetts. The troublesome lot had already chased off two Phys. Ed. teachers when James Naismith was charged with the task of finding them an indoor sport to play.

Naismith began brainstorming. It would be a game with…a large round ball. But players wouldn't be allowed to run with the ball. That way there would be no tackling and roughness. The object of the game would be…to shoot the ball into a goal box. But not with force…with accuracy, just as in the game Duck on a Rock. When Naismith played the game as a kid, skillful players had thrown rocks in an arc to knock a "duck" off a big rock. To get players to do this, he thought, the mouth of the goal should be horizontal—not vertical like in soccer.

The next morning Naismith grabbed a soccerball and asked the caretaker, Pop Stebbins, for two boxes. Stebbins had no boxes but gave Naismith some old peach baskets. Naismith nailed the peach baskets to a balcony railing at each end of the gym. The game was an instant hit and "Basket ball" bounced around the world as people everywhere began tacking up hoops. And that's how planet Earth got game.

Chapter 1

THAT'S THE WAY THE BALL BOUNCES

Ba-boom-ba!

Is any sound more exciting than that of a bouncing basketball up for grabs? Instantly, the game's a mad scramble. A loose ball is anybody's ball and everybody wants to get their hands on it.

Get it. Grab it. Catch it. Nab it any way you can. Players jump for it, lunge for it, and dive for it as both teams fight for it. Possession of the ball is half the battle in basketball, for the team with the highest score wins and neither team can score without the ball.

The orange sphere rockets all around the court in a dizzying blur. And players have to handle it "just so" to sink it in the basket for a satisfying swish. Get the inside scoop on how pros handle this jumpy character and what puts the bounce in its step.

Bounce this Way! ➤

What makes this pumped-up character so hot to handle?

IT WEARS A LEATHER JACKET

The official NBA ball sports a leather jacket that feels soft and broken-in over time. It's made of eight panels of cowhide. Thousands of tiny raised dots called pebbles cover each leather panel— 122 pebbles per square inch to be exact. The pebbles give the ball a unique grainy feel, so players can grip it firmly. And black lines called channels run between the panels to also help players get a grip.

IT'S GOT SIZE

Sitting next to a golf ball, baseball, or hockey puck, the official NBA ball looks like a giant hulk. It measures 23 cm (9 in.) across the middle and 75 cm (29 1/2 in.) around. Basketball's inventor, James Naismith, chose a large but light ball that was easy to throw and catch, in hopes the sport could be played by many people.

IT'S BRIGHT

The ball's bright orange color makes it easy to spot among a throng of players on the court. But in the early days, balls were tan-and-black or white all over. Later, home teams could choose a tan or yellow ball for games. But when basketball bounced onto TV around 1960, the NBA decided to make the ball orange so it was easier to see.

IT'S BOUNCY

Born to be bounced: that's the ball alright! It bounces as players dribble up and down the court, fire passes to teammates, and shoot off the backboard. In fact, the average basketball lives for 40,000 to 50,000 bounces before it loses its "oomph" and gets tossed out of the game for good. What's more, it must pass a bounce test to get in the game. When dropped from 1.83 m (6 ft.), the ball must bounce between 1.24 to 1.37 m (49 to 54 in.) high. That's nearly the height of a ten-year-old kid!

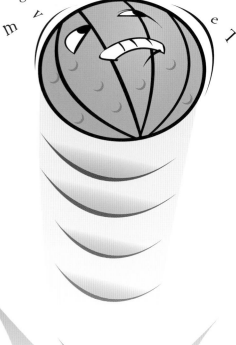

IT PLAYS UNDER PRESSURE

Life's tough at the top. The official NBA ball always plays under pressure. The Rules say the ball must be inflated with 7.5 to 8.5 pounds of air pressure. So before each and every game, the officials check that the game ball is properly inflated. If it's not, it doesn't get in the game. Here's why: a ball with too little air pressure gets soft and mushy, so it doesn't bounce as high as normal. On the other hand, a ball with too much air pressure gets hard and springy, so it bounces higher. Either way, it's chucked out of the game, so it doesn't throw players off their game.

IT'S AN "AIRHEAD"

But that doesn't mean it's dull. The air inside the ball is what makes it bounce so smartly! Here's how. Air is elastic, like a rubberband. So air allows the ball to shrink and expand during bounces. When the ball hits the floor, for example, it squashes at the point of impact as the air inside it squishes up. Then the air expands and the ball snaps back into shape, pushing down on the floor. And since for every action in our universe, there is an equal and opposite reaction, the floor pushes back, bouncing the ball up into the air. Boing!

Quick Shot

Just call Don Nelson "Sticky Fingers." The wily 1970s star of the Boston Celtics smeared Stickum, pine tar resin, on his fingers. Then when he faked shots, the sticky goo helped his fingers stick to the ball.

A CHARACTER INSIDE AND OUT

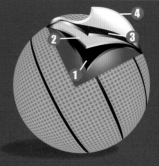

It takes four layers to make a ball that's fit for hoops handling. The innermost layer (1) is a hollow, round air sac made of butyl rubber, the same material as the inner tubes of bicycle tires. Machines inject the sac full of air then wind 2,100 m (6,890 ft.) of nylon thread (2) around it to ensure the sac keeps its shape. Next, a rubber carcass (3) is molded around the nylon-wound sac. Finally, eight panels of top-quality leather (4) are cemented onto the carcass. Tiny pebbles that have been pressed into this outer layer help players grip the ball to make their head-, er, hand-spinning moves.

BOUNCING THROUGH TIME

Check out how the ball has rolled along over the years to become the bright and bouncy character it is today.

1891

Eeny, meeny, miny, mo… "Should we play the new game with a football or a soccerball?" wonders basketball's inventor James Naismith. The football's shape makes it easy to carry on the run, he thinks, which is exactly what he doesn't want players to do. So Naismith throws up a soccerball to kick off, er, jump-start the world's first basketball game.

1894

A.G. Spalding & Brothers rolls out the world's first basketball after James Naismith asks them to make a special ball for hoops. Spalding stitches leather pieces together over a rubber inflatable bladder. Other companies soon follow. The early basketballs have raised laces (see right) and don't bounce easily or reliably. What's more, if the laces hit the rim, the ball can go for a wacky rebound anywhere. Boink!

1896

The Official Rules say the "ball shall be tightly inflated and so laced" that players can't hold it by the laces. But since the ball's size and bounciness dribbles, or varies, "all over the court," players don't know what it'll do in their hands. So a year later, the Rules set a standard ball size and quality, too.

1949

Dribbling becomes easier as the ball's lacings are removed for good. The Rules call for the ball to be made with leather panels that are not stitched together, but "cemented" to a round molded fabric that covers its airtight rubber bladder.

1967

Ha, ha! What a joke! The American Basketball Association (ABA) becomes the laughingstock of basketball when it takes to the court with a ball painted red, white, and blue. But the snickering stops once people see how good the ABA's game is. And eventually the ABA joins the NBA.

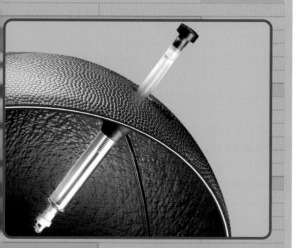

2001

Basketballs go high-tech. A newly developed built-in micropump allows officials and players to adjust the ball's air pressure on the fly without a separate needle and pump. The result? Players everywhere no longer have to put up with an under-performing, underinflated ball.

2003

The ball's character becomes more colorful. One ball manufacturer makes a ball that changes color in response to light, turning NBA-orange indoors and street-funky dark-brown outdoors. And a new black ball bounces onto the scene with glow-in-the-dark channels to brighten up night hoops.

Odd Balls, Goof Balls, and Handy Balls

Over the years, some balls have performed better than others. Which of these balls would you rather play with? Answer on page 64.

- In the early days of hoops, players couldn't always get their hands on a basketball or soccerball. So they'd chuck a football at the basket. Talk about playing in a jam.

- When women's teams from Washington and Ellensburg went head to head in 1896, the ball was anything but regular. The Ellensburg ball measured 82 cm (32 1/4 in.) all around, while the Washington ball measured 84 cm (33 1/4 in.) one way around and 86 cm (34 in.) the other! Since the Washington ball was a "Victor," the standard ball of the day, officials went with it and let the bounces fall where they may.

- One day in the 1990s, nine-year-old Christopher Haas noticed that some of his friends were having trouble making shots, because they weren't holding the ball correctly. So he dipped his hands in poster paint, marked the correct hand positions on the ball with his palm prints, and the Hands-On Basketball was born.

Grrls Get Their Own Ball

Just one month after basketball was invented, girls and women got a hold of the ball and began shooting hoops. Today, the Women's National Basketball Association (WNBA) has its very own ball. The women's ball has the same vim and vigor as the men's, plus a few unique characteristics:

It's a Tiger

The official WNBA ball roars all over the court sporting stripes, alternating orange and white leather panels.

It's Smaller

Studies show that a smaller ball is easier for smaller hands to handle. So the width, or diameter, of the WNBA ball is 2.5 cm (1 in.) less than the men's ball by design.

It's Pumped

The official WNBA ball has a built-in pump underneath its leathery skin. That way officials can add or release air "anytime anywhere," so the ball always has the proper air pressure. Talk about being pumped up and ready to go!

Psssst. Want the inside track on the riddles, secrets, and rules of handling the ball like a pro? Read on.

Oops!

The First Riddle of Hoops

Hey, all you hot hands out there. Can you solve this riddle of the game?

What makes the ball look like a yo-yo on a string, feels like playing catch with the floor, and lets players move with the ball without holding the ball?

If you said "dribbling," you're right on the ball, just like the early players who invented the clever maneuver. There was no such thing as dribbling back in 1891, when James Naismith wrote the original 13 rules of the game. The third rule out-lawed running with the ball. So when players were guarded too closely to dish it off, they had a riddle-like problem on their hands: how could they run with the ball without carrying it? It wasn't long before a few discovered that they could let go of the ball then catch it again over and over as they ran. Dribbling was born and it soon became an integral skill of the game.

Slick Dribbling

So your hot hands are burning to dribble like a pro. Well, for starters, don't think of dribbling as bouncing the ball. Think of it as playing catch with the floor. Then "throw" and "catch" the ball with your fingers not your palm. Your fingers are more sensitive than your palm, so they will give you more control of the ball. Keep your head up and don't look at the ball. Keep track of it through your fingers' sense of touch, so you can use your eyes to find open teammates or open areas to drive through on the court. Keep the ball close to your body to make it easier to control. Dribble it high to run fast. But dribble it low when you're close to opponents. The fact is, the closer to the floor the ball is, the faster it will return to you. And the less time it's out of your hands, the less likely you are to lose it!

Got

No Punching or Goaltending Allowed

Besides dribbling the ball, you can throw it or bat it. But punching and kicking it are strictly forbidden. Basketball's inventor, Naismith, ruled out these maneuvers, so that when players missed the ball, they wouldn't accidentally punch or kick an opponent in the face. Whomp! The fact is, Naismith wanted teams to succeed by skill not by roughing up their opponents. He also made it illegal to goaltend the basket. Even though defenders can block shots with their hands, once the ball's above the hoop, they cannot touch it or bat it away. These rules still stand today. Otherwise, teams could just stick a tall player or two near the basket to swat all the shots away.

Which is the bounciest ball of all? Try this experiment and see.

YOU WILL NEED

- baseball
- chalk
- tennis ball
- basketball
- wooden gym floor

1 Use the chalk to mark a line on the wall at about shoulder height.

2 Line up the bottom of the basketball with the chalk line on the wall.

3 Drop the ball onto the floor.

4 Use the chalk to mark the height of the bounce on the wall where the bottom of the ball reaches.

5 Repeat steps two to four for the baseball and tennis ball.

Which ball bounced the highest of them all? (Check your results on page 64.)

STAR ☆

Dr. J, a.k.a Julius Erving, the 1970s all-star doctor of dunk, said his secret was in his fingers. "I was born with extremely long fingers and sensitive fingertips. They let me hold the ball longer, wait until I see my opening, and then shoot with a little more control than most guys."

Julius Erving

TIP

Learn to dribble with both hands. That way you'll be twice as hard to guard. Stand on the spot and dribble the ball 30 times with each hand. Then dribble down the court with one hand and back with the other three times. Do this drill often and try switching hands on the fly in games.

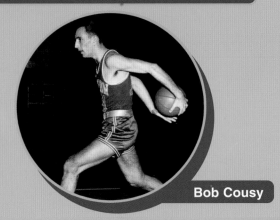

Bob Cousy

Houdini of the Hardwood

Nobody could handle the ball like Bob Cousy, the star point guard of the 1950s Boston Celtics. Cousy earned the nickname Houdini of the Hardwood, after the famous magician, because of his magical moves with the ball. With his amazing peripheral vision, he could see practically the whole court. He found open teammates with a virtual bag of tricks—no-look passes and behind-the-back feeds that had never been seen before.

What was hard to believe was that Cousy had never touched a basketball until he was 12, when he moved to a neighborhood where all the kids played hoops. Suddenly, he was hooked. He found himself playing streetball around the clock and the local competition was fierce. Cousy was cut from the school team twice!

When he was 13, Cousy fell out of a tree and broke his right arm. So what did the hoops-crazy kid do? Learn to dribble and shoot with his left, of course. And when his old coach saw him playing with both hands, he asked Cousy back to the school team. But Cousy never tried to be flashy—he just did whatever it took to make a play. And his magic moves caught on and changed the game.

Chapter 2

COURT OF ACTION

Fast and action-packed—that's what basketball is. You might say it's played in a "court of action." Players race from end to end. They snatch the ball, drive to the basket, fake past opponents, and jam the ball through the hoop—sometimes all in seconds flat!

But shooting hoops isn't only in the moves players make. While everybody knows you don't need much gear to play b-ball—only a ball and a basket (and in a pinch, a bicycle wheel rim, garbage can, or milk crate can stand in for the hoop), the playing court and equipment do affect the action of the game. In fact, as the court and equipment have developed, they've changed the way players play and the game itself. Check out what all the "hoop-la" is about.

Take a Courtside Seat! ➤

Get your ticket here. Step right up for a courtside view of how the floor, basket, and backboard go to work for players during the game.

The Score on the Floor

Pro players scoot, leap, and bound on hardwood floors often made of maple. This smooth, even surface helps the ball bounce cleanly and accurately, so players don't have to watch the ball as they dribble. Maple is strong enough to resist cracking and denting under the constant pounding of players' feet and the rock (that's hoops speak for ball). But maple is softer and more flexible than

concrete, so it has more "give." As players press down on maple to jump, the wood compresses, or slightly squashes down. Then it springs back up and pushes against players' feet, adding some of its elastic energy to players' jumps, which can bring them closer to the basket. In fact, a maple floor gives players more lift than concrete. Could it be something to jump up and down about?

Quick Shot

The average player can jump 2.5 cm (1 in.) or more higher on a wood floor than a concrete one. It might not sound like much, but it could be the difference between missing and sinking a basket.

Behind the Backboard

This see-through board holds the rim of the basket. It also helps players shoot. First off, it gives players a clear target to shoot at—a white square directly above the rim (see left). Secondly, it deflects shots into the basket. Ba-boom-swish! Players often bank shots, shooting the ball at an angle on the backboard, to direct the ball into the hoop. The backboard is made of smooth, even Plexiglass that doesn't dent. Otherwise, banked shots could take crazy bounces that could send them anywhere and everywhere but the hoop.

The Scoop on the Hoop

The next time you see a basket, take a good look. How many balls do you think can fit through the hoop, or rim, at once? Would you believe two? An NBA hoop is twice as wide as the ball. It hangs 3 m (10 ft.) above the floor, the very same height as the game's first peach baskets. The rim is made of metal and the net of flexible white cord. As the ball falls through the basket, the net slows it down. Swish! That way it's easy to tell that the shot went in and players have a moment to catch their breath. Talk about letting a shot sink in!

Shaquille O'Neal

What's the key?

It's the painted rectangle at each end of the court with the free throw circle on top. It's also known as the paint, the free throw lane, and the foul lane. The key spans 4.9 m (16 ft.) wide. But when it first appeared on the court, it was only 1.8 m (6 ft.) wide. Since it was much narrower than the circle on top back then, it looked like a key.

What makes backboards break?

Slams, jams, and dunks! When players dunk the ball through the basket with lots of force, the rim may shake and rattle. The resulting tremor can shatter the backboard. That's why the NBA uses breakaway rims—rims that detach under pressure. Otherwise, backboards might crack up regularly and delay games.

How Time Built the Court

Check out how time tooled the game into today's action-packed contest of thrills.

1891 James Naismith hangs peach baskets at each end of the YMCA gym (above), and the world's first basketball game gets underway on a floor less than half the size of NBA courts today. Naismith sends two teams of nine onto the floor at once. Talk about a traffic jam in the free throw lane!

1892 Before courts existed, players shot hoops anywhere baskets could be rigged up—outdoors, in gyms, dance halls, churches, even bars. That made basketball a hazardous sport. For as the ball flew into windows, radiators, and stairs, so did the players who tore after it. They even had the scars to prove it!

1893 Running with the ball is a no-no. Naismith's original 13 rules say players must throw the ball from the spot where

they catch it, leaving players with few options to make plays. So rulemakers allow players to turn around on the spot. This eventually becomes the pivot rule, which allows players to take one step with one foot while the other foot—the pivot foot—remains on the floor.

1894 Officials paint a free throw line in front of each basket. Now when a team gets fouled, any one of their players gets to take a shot from the line without any interference from opponents.

1895 Fans who sit near the baskets in the upper gallery, or running track, of gyms have a nasty habit of giving the home team a helping hand. They bat the home team's shots into the basket and swat the visitors' shots away. In 1895, the first backboards go up to take these "goaltenders" out of the game.

1896 Chicken wire and steel mesh cages go up around pro courts. This stops fans from being trampled by players chasing out-of-bound balls, and players from acquiring broken jaws and bruises hand-delivered by their opponents' fans. Instead, the game becomes a bloody battle as players slam each other into the cage's sharp edges. What's more, players learn how to change direction and slip by opponents by bouncing off the sides of the cage. Eventually, the cages are made of rope rather than metal, giving players some relief.

Quick Shot

When cagers held court, if a player near the cage had the ball, he might get caught like a fly. Wily opponents would grab the ropes of the cage around him, and "tie" him up! A jump ball would then be called to restart the game. So the "catchy" move caught on!

1897 Rulemakers decide five to a side is the perfect number of players to have on the court. This clears space to give players room to maneuver.

1898 Dribbling, which players have discovered lets them move with the ball, is officially allowed by the Rules.

1906 Rulemakers call for the bottom to be cut out of the basket. At first, a janitor had to climb a ladder to get the ball every time a basket was scored. Later, a small hole was cut in the bottom of the basket, and the ball poked out with a pole. By 1893, some baskets had a pull-cord to release the ball (see above). In 1906, the ball drops straight through, so players can pick it up and go.

1909 Glass replaces wood and wire backboards. This gives the ball a smooth, dent-free surface to strike, cutting down unpredictable bounces that send banked shots way off target.

1923 When teams get a free throw, they send in their best shooter for the shot. So getting a foul is practically as good as scoring. Basketball's rulemakers declare that the player who gets fouled must step up to take the shot.

1932 Officials paint a midcourt line across center court. Now, once teams get their hands on the ball, they must move it past the line into their offensive zone within ten seconds or else lose it to the opposition.

1932 The game busts out of its cage for good but basketball players are still called "Cagers."

1935 Some players like to park themselves in the best shooting position—directly under the basket. B-ball's rulemakers give them a "parking ticket," the three-second violation, which outlaws standing in the key more than three seconds.

1946 A shattered backboard delays the Boston Celtics' first game for an hour. The only spare is in another building, where a circus is performing. Legend has it that officials found the backboard covered in elephant dung! The elephant left its mark alright as the Rules soon call for a spare to be kept on site.

1954 Danny Biasone, owner of the Syracuse Nationals, invents and builds a 24-second shot clock (see page 22) to speed up the game and force players to shoot.

1971 Women's basketball introduces a 30-second shot clock, cuts back the number of players to a side from six to five, and lets them loose all over the court. Until now, women's teams have played with six players—three who had to stick to the offensive court and three to the defensive court. Why? When teacher Clara Baer had asked Naismith for a copy of his rules, he sent a court diagram showing where six players normally played. And she thought the players had to stay in those spots.

1979 Rulemakers throw the three-point shot into the NBA. Now when players sink a basket from beyond 7.2 m (23 ft. 9 in.), a.k.a. the three-point line, they rack up three points.

1996 The Women's National Basketball Association (WNBA) sets up court. Finally women have a chance to play pro ball.

HOME-COURT ADVANTAGE

Does home-court advantage really exist? You bet! Studies show that basketball teams play better at home than away. But seeking that advantage wasn't always "above board." Check out some tricks home teams have used to trip up opponents.

Floored by Dead Spots

Legend has it that the floor of Boston Garden, the Celtics' old home, was riddled with dead spots—areas where the ball would "drop dead" instead of bouncing back up. Built during a wood shortage after World War II, the floor was made of wood scraps that fit together like a jigsaw puzzle. Opponents believed the Celtics maneuvered visiting players to the dead spots to steal the ball. Some former Celtics say they did use the floor advantage. Others say there was no advantage whatsoever—they never knew where the spots would be because the floor was put together differently every night. Still, former Celtics coach Red Auerbach once said, "If [other] teams felt it was a poor floor, I used it for an advantage by playing with their minds." How's that for flooring your opponents?

Stiffed by the Rim?

The Chicago Bulls hadn't won a game at the Detroit Pistons' Palace in eons. When Bulls' coach Phil Jackson watched Pistons' game tapes to prepare for a matchup in 1991, he noticed something strange: the rim near the Pistons' bench was stiffer than the rim at the other end of the court. So shots that weren't right on target were more likely to bounce off the rim than go in.

It's no secret that games are often won or lost in the final minutes. So Jackson varied his routine. He chose to shoot at the stiff rim for the first half instead of the second. And the Bulls won the game!

Caught Off Guard by Nets

A net's a net, right? Wrong. Some nets are looser or tighter than others. While that may sound like a small thing, it can give teams precious seconds to get a jump on their opponents. Here's how: a loose net lets the ball drop through more quickly than normal. So home teams can install loose nets to speed up the pace of the game. Then by retrieving the ball faster than opponents expect, they may be able to outrun their opponents to score on them. On the other hand, a tight net releases the ball more slowly than normal. It "catches" the ball briefly. And this can give home teams a moment to set up defensive positions before their opponents get the ball and move down court to shoot. Either way, loose or tight nets can throw a wrench into the visiting teams' game.

The Harlem Globetrotters Rule the Court

The Harlem Globetrotters have never needed home-court advantage to win. In fact, they started out with a reputation for walking onto opponents' home turf and blowing them away. The team formed in 1926 in Chicago—not Harlem!—from a core of players who were the first all-black team to win the city's high school basketball championship. They soon began barnstorming, or traveling from town to town, to play serious basketball against the local competition. But back then, many towns didn't want to book them because they were black. So they hired a white manager, Abe Saperstein, who succeeded in changing all that. Saperstein named the team the Harlem Globetrotters and gave them their trademark red, white, and blue uniforms. The Globetrotters then went on a tear, thrashing teams everywhere. But, as Saperstein soon realized, local fans didn't enjoy watching their team get completely routed. So he encouraged the Globetrotters to clown around and entertain the crowd once they racked up a comfortable lead. And that's how the team developed their awesome dropkicks from center court, dazzling dribble displays, player-boosts to the shoulders to score, and lose-the-ball-under-my-shirt routines, which made them a hot ticket all over the world.

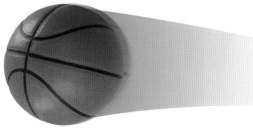

Quick Answers to Speedy Questions

What's an air ball?
A shot that misses the basket completely, hitting only air. Phffffft! The trick is to not let it deflate your spirit.

What's a hot hand?
A player who seems to have the "right" touch on the ball and sinks lots of baskets.

The 24-Second Clock

Saved in the Nick of Time

"**W**hat a bore! The game was a snore!" That's what you might have heard from fans in 1950. The action was mindnumbingly slow and scoring extremely low as NBA teams with the lead sat on the ball without shooting, to let the clock run out.

On November 22, 1950, scoring sunk to an all-time low as the Fort Wayne Pistons squeaked by the Minneapolis Lakers, 19 to 18. The fans booed, threw trash on the court, and sprung out of the stands to go after the players at the end of the game.

Soon fans everywhere stopped going to the snooze-a-thons altogether. So in 1954, Danny Biasone, owner of the Syracuse Nationals, invented a "wake-up call"—the 24-second shot clock. Once a team got the ball, if they didn't shoot within 24 seconds, an alarm buzzed and they had to give the ball to their opponents. Why the magic number 24? Biasone figured two teams should average 120 shots a game. So he divided 120 shots into the number of seconds in a game—2,880—and got 24. That meant one shot every 24 seconds.

Scoring shot up immediately and so did fans' interest. The shot clock set the pace for today's fast-action, high-scoring contests, which are often a battle till the final buzzer. It saved the game in the nick of time!

Chapter 3

GAME WEAR

Hot and itchy! That's what the first basketball uniforms were in the 1890s. Men wore short-sleeved jerseys and long trousers made of wool that likely left them sopping wet with sweat as they ran up and down the court. And women didn't have it much better as they chased the ball in long-sleeved dresses past their knees— and bloomers. What's more, the shoes those men and women wore were nothing like the cool marvels of engineering you drool over today. Players were slip-sliding away in standard gym shoes whose soft leather soles had no traction!

It wasn't long before basketball players realized that sleeves held their arms back from shooting, and their heavy uniforms slowed them down on the court. So those clunky sets of game wear soon gave way to sleeveless tops and shorts. And eventually shoes were made just for hoops. Get the inside scoop on how basketball uniforms and sneakers stepped up and got in the game!

Cool Threads Ahead! ➤

C heck out how the uniforms pros wear today go to work on the court.

1 Jersey

Pros pull on loose-fitting jerseys to play. Oversize armholes give their arms lots of room to shoot, catch, and pass the ball. Lightweight, breathable fabric lets air flow in and out to cool players down as they heat up, and wicks away moisture to keep them dry as they sweat during the action of the game.

2 Shorts

Basketball shorts are made of breathable polyester or nylon mesh. Today, baggy shorts have replaced the tight, short-shorts that pros wore up to the 1980s. And they aren't just a matter of style. When players lean over to catch their breath between plays, long shorts stop their sweaty palms from slipping off their legs.

3 Socks

Pros wear soft, thick socks for cushioning. Official NBA socks are made with acrylic, an artificial woollike fiber. Acrylic helps prevent blisters and it wicks, or carries away, sweat from players' feet. Some pros wear long socks, some short ones, and others wear two pairs at once. It's a matter of individual style.

Quick Shot

Some pros break out a new pair of kicks as often as every three games! Good thing used shoes can be ground up and recycled into courts and padding under hardwood b-ball floors.

4 Shoes

Basketball shoes provide stability and cushioning, flex under pressure, and absorb shocks as players jump, leap, pivot, and suddenly stop or start. The shoes have three main parts (see inset). Many pros wear high-tops for ankle support. Others prefer lighter mid-tops or low-tops.

5 The Laces

Laces help keep feet secure during quick stops, starts, turns, and moves from side to side. Sometimes the laces are hidden for a sleek look. Some kicks have zippers or velcro instead, while others have a combination of laces and an ankle strap for added ankle support and stability.

6 The Upper

This is the top of the shoe. Made of soft, light synthetic materials and mesh, it's designed to hold players' feet in place and let their feet breathe.

7 The Midsole

Like its name suggests, the midsole sits between the upper and the outsole. This soft, shock-absorbing layer is the most important part of a basketball shoe. It's designed and made with materials to give players' feet a boost as they blast off the floor to shoot or grab the ball.

8 The Outsole

Made of polyurethane foam or rubber, the outsole is the bottom of the shoe. Its flat, wide base gives players stability. The outsole often has a herringbone–patterned tread, which is designed for basketball action to give players traction. That way players' feet don't slide out from under them as they tear about the court.

TIP

Gear up like a pro. Wear a mouthpiece to protect your pearly whites, a headband to keep sweat out of your eyes, and wristbands to keep your hands dry for handling the ball.

Quick Answers to Speedy Questions

What are warm-up suits?
Between warm-up and play, long pants and jackets keep pros' muscles warm and raring to go.

DRESSED TO HOOP

Uniforms Get "Shipshape"

In the early 1900s, women played in middy blouses that had sailor collars and bloomers. Back then some people thought basketball was just a sport for women, and even called it a "sissy" game. As if!

Padded for Protection

When games were played in wire cages (see page 18) in the early 1900s, blood flowed freely on the court as players slammed each other into the wire, which often cut their skin. So players scrambled for any protection they could get. In fact, padded pants, kneepads, and elbow pads were all part of the standard uniform.

A Winning 'Do

Dennis Rodman (left), star rebounder in the 1990s, wasn't the first player to grace the court with rainbow-colored hair. In 1936, the first women's pro basketball team all colored their hair red. They called themselves the All American Red Heads and hit the road, daring men's teams all over to matchups, playing by men's rules.

TIME'S KICKS PICKS

Step through time and check out how shoe designers have used different technologies to put pep in players' steps.

1903 The first pair of basketball shoes with suction soles are unveiled. The soles are designed for traction and "guaranteed not to slip even on a dancing floor." Depending on the model, a pair costs anywhere from $1 to $4!

1916 The first sneakers steal into the world. Canvas shoes with a rubber sole quietly appear on masses of people's feet. Legend has it that an ad executive called the shoes "sneakers," because their rubber soles allowed people to sneak around without making a sound.

1916 A canvas "high top" walks into the sneaker market. A few years later, pro baller Chuck Taylor is signed to endorse the shoes. Taylor helps redesign the tread for more traction and suggests an ankle patch to protect players' ankles. He sells the improved shoes out of the trunk of his car, and they become the number one choice of basketball players everywhere for more than 60 years.

1972 Bill Bowerman, a former track coach, pours rubber into a waffle iron in his kitchen. And lo and behold, a waffle sole pops out that gives runners phenomenal traction and becomes a runaway best seller.

1976 Teenage runner John Hoke cuts up a pair of worn-out shoes to see how they work and a brainwave hits him: why not pump air into sneaker soles? He sketches out his idea and sends it to a running shoe manufacturer, who is already developing the radical idea.

1979 Pockets of pressurized air are injected into the midsole of running shoes. Runners lace them up and feel as if they are bouncing on air. But it takes four years to figure out how to put air in hoop shoes, because basketball players need stability not bounciness.

1984 Michael Jordan, third pick of the NBA draft, signs a sneaker deal and wears "Air Jordans" on the court. His play virtually takes flight. Is it his amazing ability that lifts him head and shoulders above all other pros, people wonder, or the shoes?

1999 A basketball shoe that has a heel cushion of helium gas appears. The idea is that helium, which is lighter than air, will make the shoes lighter to give players more lift and buoyancy to leap above the rim. But the shoes don't make much of an impression. They seem to disappear into thin air just like, well, a helium balloon. Poof!

2000 Boing! A shoe 16 years in the making bounds onto the court with "springs" attached to its sole. The springs are columns made of a durable foam found in Formula One race cars. They not only add spring to players' steps, but work as shock absorbers as players zoom all over the court.

TIP

Looking for the right basketball shoes for you? Have your foot measured in the store to determine your proper foot size. Then try on several pairs and test them out. Walk around, jog, and make some quick stops and starts. Whichever pair feels the most comfortable is the pair for you.

The Next Step

What will shoe designers think of next? Injecting kicks with rocket fuel or Mexican jumping beans? It's really anybody's guess. But experts say the future of shoe design lies in personalizing shoes. That means shoe companies will give the average cool customer the means to choose the style and performance elements to create their very own personal shoe. Sounds like the perfect fit!

Quick Shot

Around the late 1940s, pro ballers made one or two pairs of shoes last a whole season long. The Boston Celtics wore only white sneakers back then. But when coach Red Auerbach noticed how quickly their shoes got dirty, he had the team switch to black. And black hoop shoes soon became a symbol of the Celtics' cutthroat style.

DESIGNING THE NEXT "SHOE-IN"

Oooh! Where'd you get those cool kicks? Just how do shoe designers come up with the latest pair of "gotta-haves" designed to take basketball players to new heights? Would you believe they start with a vision in their heads and end up consulting kids on the street? Check out all the steps they take from start to finish.

Starting Blocks: The Imagination

Inspiration for new shoe designs often springs from the imagination. What if we could pump hoop shoes full of air? What if a shoe were hyper-light but loaded with protection for players' feet? Or what if we could put springs in shoes? Designers ask themselves questions like these then head to the lab to try out their ideas—no matter how crazy or ridiculous they might sound!

In the Lab

Designers work with scientists and engineers to build prototypes of their designs. Sometimes, they begin by videotaping and studying all the motions basketball players make. That way they understand exactly what the shoe has to do. Then once they have a prototype that they think can do all that, they invite players to the lab to test them out.

On Pros' Feet

The players put the shoes through the paces on treadmills and a hardwood basketball floor while the designers and scientists watch each step. High-speed video cameras record players' every move, sensors wired to their skin measure their muscle activity, and pressure sensors in the shoes measure the forces on the shoes and their feet. Designers then feed all this data into a computer to figure out how well their shoes perform under the typical pressures of the game.

Test 'n' Tweak

Based on what the test results reveal, designers may rebuild designs, tweak them, or go back to the drawing board altogether. For example, if pressure sensors reveal a lot of pressure behind players' big toes, designers may put more cushioning in that part of the shoe. Then they'll test the new design and rebuild or tweak it until they're satisfied. The ongoing challenge is to strike the perfect balance between cushioning and stability.

On the Street

The work of shoe designers doesn't stop with pros' feet. Designers also take their prototypes to kids for feedback. While pro players help designers cool a shoe for performance and style, kids help them inject the cool factor. The fact is, there are a lot more kids to sell shoes to than basketball pros. So shoe companies take their prototypes to kids in big cities. And if kids give them a thumbs down, the shoe doesn't get off the ground without a makeover!

Superstar Treatment

In the case of a signature shoe designed for a superstar, designers build in technical features to enhance the star's playing style. Take dunker supreme Vince Carter, for example. When Nike wanted to make a shoe with Vince's name on it, they worked with him to find a design that would help him leap off the floor and go higher. Shoe designer Aaron Cooper used a "jump sock" to give Vince cushioning and ankle support. "This foot cradle helps Vince do what he does best—jump," said Cooper. The design incorporated Nike Shox "springs" underneath the whole foot instead of just the heel as in other Shox models. And inspiration for the design came from Vince's favorite car, the Bentley, a luxury car known for performance. Now that's superstar treatment alright!

Are hoop shoes really worth the mega bucks they cost? First, since shoe companies put out a dozen new pairs of basketball shoes every three months, kicks are practically out of date as soon as you take them out of the box. Who can keep up? Second, just because your favorite player plays well in a certain kind of shoes, doesn't mean you will, too. You may have a completely different style of playing, not to mention a different pair of feet. And third, shoe companies often give the shoe's performance features fancy names to make the features seem bigger and better than they really are. Despite any company's claims, it's not the shoes that make the plays—it's your feet inside them. It's you who's got game. So only you can decide how much you're willing to fork over for new kicks.

Sheryl Swoopes

Swooping In Feet First

When Sheryl Swoopes was seven, she began playing with her older brothers who often turfed her off the court because she was a girl. In high school, Sheryl hung around the gym to play with the guys, but could rarely get in the game.

"It didn't matter how good I was," Sheryl told the magazine *Sports Illustrated*. "It was always, 'You're a girl. You can't play with the guys.'" But that only motivated Sheryl to get better and better. In 1993, Sheryl led her college team to a championship victory, racking up 47 points in the final game in a record-setting performance among college women—and men.

The catlike quick player who pounced on the hoop for slam dunks was being called the female Michael Jordan. Nike made Sheryl the first woman to have a signature shoe: Air Swoopes. So Sheryl had shoes—but no game.

Back then, there was no pro women's basketball in North America after college. Sheryl worked as a bank teller until the U.S. Women's National Team began training for the 1996 Olympics. That's when women's hoops took flight. The U.S. women won the gold medal. And the WNBA formed on the heels of the victory, signing Sheryl as its first player. Then girls everywhere could dream of playing in her shoes.

Chapter 4

THE COMPLETE ATHLETE

Zip! They sprint down the court, cut across the paint, and leap up to catch passes. Then they dodge past opponents, spring off both feet, and bury the rock down the hoop. And once they knock it down, the rock automatically goes to their opponents. Then basketball players quickly switch to defense, trying to steal the ball, block shots, and box out opponents. Is it any wonder they need to be in tip-top physical condition?

Basketball's intense bursts of action burn up lots of physical energy quickly. So pros train all year round to develop their strength, speed, and conditioning. Plus, they practice skills such as shooting and passing over and over, and run through team maneuvers until they can practically do them in their sleep. Pros also train their minds just like they train their bodies.

Get the skinny on what it takes to compete as a complete b-ball athlete.

Shape Up! ➤

THE BODY

Getting into first-rate playing shape is a big job. For starters, the average NBA-er stands 2.01 m (6 ft. 7 in.) tall and weighs 102 kg (224 lbs.)! What's more, their size doesn't mean a thing unless they have the strength, speed, and basketball skills to rev it up.

Train to Gain

Train, train, and train some more. That's the way pro basketball players whip their bodies into shape. Each player has an individual training program designed to maximize his or her playing potential. They work on cardiorespiratory fitness—the ability of the heart and lungs to deliver blood, oxygen, and nutrients to working muscles and body tissue. And they develop their athletic skills: strength, speed, power, flexibility, and agility.

At each training session, pros warm up their muscles as they do for games by jogging, cycling, or skipping rope. Then they stretch out their muscles. That way they develop flexibility and their muscles are less likely to tear as they workout.

They also practice, practice, and practice basketball skills, such as shooting, dunking, and making free throws. Their goal is to strengthen their muscles without losing any nimbleness to sprint about the court.

They pass the ball, drive to the basket, and run through offensive and defensive team plays. Pros also run, jog, sprint, and cycle to develop endurance. That way they can go the distance and still deliver their best performance in a game's final moments.

Taking the Leap

Pros jump over boxes, do box runs, and hop over towels. Sound crazy? Plyometric exercises like these shown below help players develop speed, agility, and explosive power. They also help increase players' vertical leap and jumping ability—exactly what players need for jump shots, shot blocks, and monster jams.

Quick Shot

Basketball is really draining. Players can lose as much as 1 to 2 litres (1/4 to 1/2 gallon) of water in sweat every hour! And if players get dehydrated like this, they tire easily and are prone to mental mistakes. So pro teams encourage their players to drink lots of fluids.

The Fuel

What do pros fuel up with to jump and leap above the rim? Rocket fuel? Nope. (They are human after all!) Try a high-energy diet of carbohydrates, proteins, and fats from a variety of foods. Experts say the following "pro-portions" can help players perform at their peak and even prevent injuries:

60 to 70% carbohydrates—Breads, cereals, pasta, fruits, and veggies fuel up players' muscles for games and practices. These carbohydrate-rich foods are players' number one source of energy.

15 to 25% fats—Fats from red meat, butter, salad dressing, milk, cheese, eggs, nuts, and seeds kick in to supply energy once players' carbohydrate energy runs out.

15 to 18% proteins—Proteins from beef, chicken, grains, nuts, and seeds help players' bodies grow and repair tissues.

Pros try to eat light pre-game meals that won't slow them down on the court. And once they find one that does the trick, they often eat the exact same thing at the exact same time before each and every game. Sound mental? Maybe it is, because pre-game rituals like this often help players mentally prepare for games. And, hey, if a meal hits the spot, so players can hit the mark, they stick with it!

Wham! Two players collide as they scramble for the ball. Whomp! A player jumps up for the rebound and lands on an opponent's foot. Basketball is a contact sport alright as players routinely crash into each other and the floor. So injuries are part of the game. Check out how training and sports medicine are helping players recover faster and better than ever before.

Rankled by an Ankle

What's the number one injury basketball pros suffer from? Sprained ankles? You bet! The irksome damage often occurs when players jump up then land on another player's foot, or roll onto the side of their own foot. Either way, it becomes a real pain.

Players may feel a pop or a tear as the ligaments, or connective tissue, around the ankle bones overstretch or even rip. Ouch! The ankle may hurt too much to walk on and swell up to the size of a tennis ball.

But thanks to expert treatment, (W)NBA players can recover much faster from ankle sprains than the average Joe or Jane—sometimes in just a few days. First off, the team's trainer and medical staff tend to the ankle right away before it has a chance to swell. They R.I.C.E. it and check for any broken bones. Say

what? R.I.C.E. it? That's R for resting it, I for icing it to keep the swelling down, C for compressing it with supportive bandages, and E for elevating it above the player's heart.

Trainers also work with players to prevent ankle injuries. They help players strengthen their ankles through specific exercises. And before practices and games, trainers wrap players' ankles with adhesive tape to keep the ankle stable. They fit some players with ankle braces instead and still others with both tape and braces for double protection. Believe it or not, an NBA team trainer tapes some 2,200 ankles a season and uses up 45 km (28 mi.) of wrap and tape!

Chilling on Ice

How do pros like Shaquille O'Neal and Chamique Holdsclaw recover from grueling games and muscle strains? Hop into an ice bath and chill out. No joke! When players give their muscles a vigorous workout in strenuous games, syrupy lactic acid builds up inside the muscles, which makes them feel tired and sore. And sitting in a tub of ice is the perfect antidote. As the ice cools players' leg muscles, for example, it tightens up the blood vessels. This drains blood out of the leg muscles along with the lactic acid. Then new, energizing blood flows into the muscles, giving players "fresh legs" for the next game. Talk about a cool recovery!

Too Rough and Rowdy 4U?

When basketball first bounced on the scene, people said it was too physically demanding for young people, especially girls. But when scientific studies put this theory to the test, the results showed that basketball wasn't harmful to players' health. Still, many parents, teachers, and doctors thought it was too rough and rowdy for girls. So to give girls the chance to play, women teachers and coaches adapted the rules to emphasize participation rather than winning. That way basketball became "ladylike" enough for girls to play in the early 1900s. Today, society's attitudes have changed and women's rules are virtually the same as men's.

Quick Shot

One research study showed that players wearing shoes with air cells were 4.3 times more likely to injure an ankle than players without air cells.

THE MIND

Imagine this: it's the final game of the (W)NBA playoffs. The score is tied in the fourth quarter with just seconds left. The team that wins the game wins the championship. A teammate intercepts a pass and dishes you the ball. Two defenders step in your path like roadblocks. You shake and bake, faking this way and that, and suddenly you're past them. The basket's in clear sight. Can you make the shot?

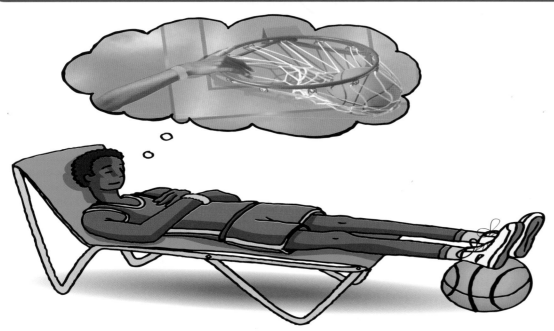

Quick Shot

One free-throw study among college students who were not basketball players showed that mental rehearsal is almost as effective as physical practice. The students who physically practiced free throws improved by 24% and those who rehearsed mentally improved by 23%. Mindblowing, or what?

Quick Answers to Speedy Questions

Flex Your "Mental Muscle"

It takes mental toughness to come through in the clutch and score when a game or championship is on the line. Pro players train their minds like they train their bodies. They learn to visually concentrate on the ball, the basket, teammates, and opponents. That way their brains focus on the visual information they need to direct the body's next move rather than any negative thoughts or doubts that can tie the body in knots.

Pros also use their minds to practice physical moves. It's called mental rehearsal, or visualization. Players choose a play they want to work on, such as faking past an opponent or driving to the basket. Then they relax and imagine themselves making the moves. The idea is that by "seeing" and "feeling" themselves perform the play successfully, they will instinctively make the winning play in similar game situations.

Why do experts call basketball a mental game?

To get the edge on an opponent, basketball players constantly have to size up situations, decide what to do, and do it quickly. The mind has to take in information from the eyes, ears, and other senses, process the information instantly like a computer, then direct the body. So the more alert the mind is, the faster it can mobilize the body to blow by an opponent.

In the Dumps with a Slump?

So, you're a sharp-shooter but lately you just can't seem to knock it down. None of your shots are going in. You've fallen into a slump. Sooner or later, it happens even to the game's top superstars.

Here's one way it can start. Say you miss a shot. Maybe your muscles are tight or you're tired. Or maybe you're not focused on the target like usual or you're thinking about a past mistake or future play instead of the present shot. Or maybe an opponent is in your face, trying to distract you or make you hurry the shot.

Whatever the case may be, you start thinking you've lost your shooting touch. And before you know it all your shots are bricks. You've plunged into a mental tail-spin and sunk into a slump.

What now? Pros climb out of slumps by focusing their minds on the physical and mental fundamentals of shooting. They also replace any negative thoughts with positive thoughts. For example, if they find themselves thinking about a missed shot, they imagine themselves putting the ball through the hoop instead. Maybe they should call it wish-ful thinking!

Quick Shot

The odds of a U.S. high school player making it to the NBA are about 7,600 to 1. And the U.S. produces most of the NBA's players. So if you come from another country, like Canadian Steve Nash (see right), the odds stacked against you are way higher.

STAR ☆

The forward who led the Boston Celtics to three NBA championships in the 1980s could "read" the game like no other. Bird often anticipated what would happen one or two moves ahead in the game. This "head-start" helped him out-smart the competition.

Larry Bird

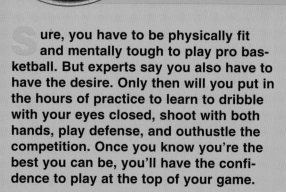

Gotta Have Heart

Sure, you have to be physically fit and mentally tough to play pro basketball. But experts say you also have to have the desire. Only then will you put in the hours of practice to learn to dribble with your eyes closed, shoot with both hands, play defense, and outhustle the competition. Once you know you're the best you can be, you'll have the confidence to play at the top of your game.

Take star point guard Steve Nash (above). When Steve was 13, he decided that he wanted to play in the NBA. From then on, he always tried to have a ball in hand and to shoot hoops as much as he could. Steve practiced 200 free throws and as many as 500 jump shots at a go! He worked hard throughout high school and college to improve every aspect of his game. And against incredible odds, Steve made it to the NBA to play the game he loves.

Michael Jordan

When Michael Jordan Didn't Make the Cut

Some people called him MJ, others called him "Air Jordan," and still others called him "His Airness." But almost everyone agreed that Michael Jordan was the greatest basketball player who ever lived. When the stellar shooting guard played for the Chicago Bulls in the 1980s and 90s, his amazing athleticism and phenomenal skills came together to lift him into a universe all his own above the rim.

What made Michael such a complete athlete who played head and shoulders above the heap? Sheer determination, lots of practice, and guts. When Michael tried out for his high school varsity team, he didn't make the cut. "I went through the day numb," he once said. But even though he was crushed, he didn't give up. "My disappointment became my determination," he said.

The coach who cut him saw Michael's potential, for he began picking him up every morning at 6:30 to work on his ballhandling, shooting, and game skills. "Basketball became more than a sport," said Michael. "It became a love and a passion, an overpowering force in my life, that to this day, drives me, moves me, and motivates me."

Chapter 5

THE SCIENCE OF EXPLOSIVE MOVES

Va-voom!

A shooter blasts into the air like a rocket to let a jump shot fly. Swat! A defender vaults with both hands up to block an incoming shot like a wall. Slam dunk! An airborne player stuffs the ball down the hoop as if to say, "This is my shot, dude. It's going in and there's absolutely nothing any-one can do about it!" Ping! A player snaps a quick pass to a teammate who zooms down the court for a shot on an unguarded basket. Swish!

What makes jump shots, shot blocks, dunks, and passes so explosive? The energy that players fire into them. Find out exactly how these moves electrify the game and bring fans to their feet with a roar. Whoo-hoo!

Blast Off! ➤

A player leaps up to catch a pass. Ka-foomp! She lands in a triple threat stance, fakes to her right, then fakes to her left. And before her opponent knows what's up, her feet blast off the ground and she pops the rock. Whoosh! Check out the split-second mechanics of a jump shot, or "J," and find out why it's the most-fired shot in the (W)NBA.

Be a Triple Threat

As with all shots and on-court moves, the player begins from b-ball's triple threat position, where she can shoot, pass, or dribble. Her feet are shoulder-width apart, knees bent, and her hands hold the ball under her chin with her elbows in. That way she's set to move any which way, and her opponents can't guess what she's about to do next.

Square Up and Line Up

To move her hands into shooting position, she turns the ball so her shooting hand is under and behind the ball. She squares her shoulders with the basket. That way she's facing the target and she can aim and control the shot. And she lines up her shooting elbow with the basket.

Coil Like a Spring

She uses her legs to power up the shot—not her arms. Experts call this "shooting with the knees." She bends her knees, coiling her legs like springs. As she brings the ball above her head, she pushes off the floor with her feet, uncoiling her legs, which boost her into the air like rocket launchers. Vroom!

Quick Shot

Jump shots are the pros' number one shot. They extend players' height briefly without warning. That way players can surprise opponents, see the hoop better, and shoot over opponents' heads.

Release the Ball

the very top of her jump, she eases the ball. She moves her balce hand a bit out of the way and ks her wrist to roll the ball off her gers. Her fingertips thrust the ball and out.

Follow Through

e continues moving her wrist forrd as if she's reaching into a cookar and she completely straightens her arm. Then she lands on her t again in the triple threat position follow her shot for a rebound.

Jumpin' Joe Makes the Jumper Go

Just Hanging Around?

Ever noticed how long pros hang in the air to take a shot? Chances are your favorite player's hang time is a lot less than it looks. Scientific studies show that the best jumpers stay airborne for only a second or less. But the moves players make, such as spinning completely around or dunking the ball over their heads, create the illusion they're hanging out much longer.

Back in the 1940s, the jump shot was anything but common. In fact, the jumper was frowned upon. Coaches thought any player who left both his feet to shoot was looking for trouble. Maybe that's because most players couldn't jump very well back then. No joke! Most players usually shot two-handed set shots with both feet planted firmly on the floor. But Joe Fulks (shooter, above) didn't let that hold him down. The high-flying Philadelphia Warrior leapt high in the air to knock it down. Jumpin' Joe thought that by jumping high he could hang in the air longer than his defenders to get a clear shot. It certainly enabled him to score. Jumpin' Joe soon led the league in scoring and the jumper began shooting up all over the league.

STAR ☆

What makes Vince Carter so explosive? When the star guard akes to the air, he can ink a jump shot, jam the all through the hoop, or woop in for an alleyoop—catch a pass in nidair and dunk it. Now hat's dynamite alright!

Vince Carter

THE EXPLOSIVE SCIENCE OF PASSING

Hey, Speedy! You've got the ball and you're covered. But your teammate's wide open. Quick! Think fast: what's the quickest way to get the ball to your teammate? Pass it? You bet!

The Proof Is in the Passing

A pass will deliver the ball faster than you or any other player can dribble or even sprint down the court. And you don't have to take anyone's word for it. Here's how to prove it. Stand on the midcourt line with a couple of teammates and ask another teammate to stand on the foul line. Have your teammate at the foul line say, "On your mark, get set, go!" then pass him the ball as your other teammates sprint to the foul line. Run through this experiment a couple of times. Notice how the pass reaches the foul line before each and every one of your teammates every time—even if you give them a head start?

YOUR SECRET WEAPON

Think of a pass as a secret weapon you can use to cut through your opponents' defense. Check out some of the passes pros launch from their on-court arsenal.

Bounce Pass

When a defender might come between the passer and receiver, players opt for the bounce pass. They make the same motions as a chest pass and aim the ball to a spot on the floor two-thirds of the way toward the receiver. The ball will pass under the defender and bounce up toward the receiver's hips.

Chest Pass

Players fire this pass when no defenders or other obstacles stand between them and the receiver. They hold the ball at chest level, step toward the receiver, and snap the ball toward the receiver's chest with a flick of their wrists.

Overhead Pass

Pros use this pass to try to confuse defenders. They often fake a chest pass, then quickly raise their arms above their heads and snap their wrists to launch the ball over defenders' heads to the receiver.

Pssst, Speedy

Here's another question for you. Suppose each of these passes is traveling at the same speed. Which one will reach the receiver the fastest?
See answer page 64.

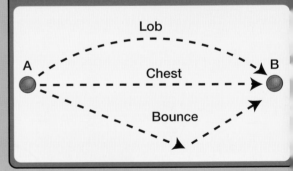

Quick Shot

When players do a sneaky play called the "backdoor," the ball handler passes the ball to one player while another fakes away from the hoop and then cuts sharply to the hoop to receive a quick pass for a layup or dunk.

42

So you want to sharpen your passes, steals, and catches? Play Monkey in the Middle. No joke! This game drills all three skills at once. No budding b-ball star can afford to pass it up!

YOU WILL NEED

• 2 friends   • a basketball

1 Have one player be the monkey in the middle, who tries to steal the ball as the other two pass it to each other.

2 When the monkey gets the ball, the monkey trades places with the player who made the pass.

Passers: make overhead, chest, and bounce passes and use fakes to keep the monkey guessing.

Monkeys: try to read each pass. Is the passer looking where he's aiming the ball, for example?

Receivers: Jump up slightly and receive the ball with both hands, letting your arms "give" a little.

Quick Answers to Speedy Questions

What's a baseball pass?

It's a pass thrown overhead with one hand like a catcher throws a baseball. The pass travels a long distance from one end of the court to the other. The barnstorming Troy Trojans invented it in the early 1900s, sparking basketball's first fast break—rush on an opponent's basket to try to score before the opponents can get there to defend it.

STAR ☆

It must be magic. That's what fans and players thought in the 80s as the 2.06 m (6 ft. 9 in.) point guard zinged no-look passes, behind-the-back dishes, and half-court feeds to teammates all over the court. It was as if Magic could pass the ball right through opposing players!

Earvin "Magic" Johnson

THE SHOT BLOCK

You're guarding an opponent who has the ball and you're doing your utmost to pressure his shot. You're keeping your body between him and the rim, holding one hand up to obstruct a clear shot, and dishing out verbal pressure by yelling "Shot." Nevertheless, your opponent jumps up to shoot. What's your last line of defense? Until Bill Russell stunned a shooter with the first shot block in the 1950s, there was none. Check out the moves of this explosive maneuver.

Anticipate the Fake

The defender watches her opponent closely for fakes this way or that. She doesn't jump until her opponent's feet leave the ground. Otherwise, she runs the risk of being lured out of position, allowing her opponent to slip by for an uncontested layup or dunk.

Jump to Block

The defender jumps up in front of the shooter and raises her hands over her head to block the shot. Smack! She's careful to jump straight up, without leaning or reaching over the shooter. That way she may squelch the ball in the shooter's hands, or bat it out of the air once it leaves the shooter's hands, or deflect it to a teammate without getting a foul.

Land to Play

Finally, the defender lands in the triple threat position ready to spring to action on the court.

How Blocked Opponents Go Mental

Psssst. Want to know how pro shot blockers make opponents go mental? They don't try to block each and every shot. Otherwise, they'd zap all their energy. What's more, their blocks would lose effect, because their opponents would expect them all the time. So pros make the shot blocks they think will have the most effect. For example, if an opponent drives to the basket thinking he's got a sure dunk, a shot blocker may step in and deny the shot altogether. And if the shot blocker does that a few choice times, his opponents may think twice about driving to the basket again. Then those shot blocks will have turned into mental blocks that stop opponents even before they get started. Whoa!

Running a Fast Break

When a pro blocks a shot or grabs a rebound under his basket, look out for a fast break. His team may explode into their opponents' end, zooming all the way to the basket before the opponents can get there to defend it. Pros ignite fast breaks by swatting or dishing the ball to a teammate as other teammates hotfoot it down the court. Fast breaks help teams rack up easy points and get ahead in the game.

★ STAR ☆

Just call Manute Bol (10) a human wall. When the 2.31-m (7-ft.-7-in.) shot blocker raised his arms over his head, almost no one could shoot over him. In 1985–86, Manute became the first rookie to lead the NBA in blocked shots, stopping a whopping 397 shots in 80 games.

Manute Bol

TIP

When you block a shot, try to angle your body or hand to deflect the ball to a teammate. That way your team can gain possession of the ball, and it's less likely to go out of bounds—and right back into your opponents' hands.

Julius Erving

Dr. J Operates on the Hoop

When Julius Erving took to the air, there was no telling what he might do above the rim. The star forward, a.k.a. Dr. J, had a flair for hanging in the air and creating spectacular layups and dunks that had never been done before.

Nevertheless, in 1976, at the now-defunct American Basketball Association's first Annual Slam-Dunk contest, Dr. J faced some tough competition. Artis Gilmore went up first with a ball in each hand and dunked one then the other through the hoop. George Gervin slammed a coiled snake, wrapping his whole right arm around the ball then uncoiling it so the ball rolled down his arm, off his fingers, and into the basket. Larry Kenon jammed a rim-shaker. Then fly guy David Thompson spun toward the hoop and dunked the ball with a force that seemed to rock the crowd right out of their seats.

But that didn't knock Dr. J off his game. The 2.01-m (6-ft.-7-in.) player stood at the foul line and took ten steps back. Then he exploded. He ran to the foul line and went airborne. Dr. J windmilled the ball and released it with surgical precision, knifing it through the hoop. Slam-DUNK! No one had ever seen anything like it. Dr. J blew all the competition away and touched down as the greatest doctor of dunk to ever operate on the hoop.

Chapter 6

HOW PROS MEASURE UP

Yo Dude!

How's the air up there? It's hard not to wonder. After all, pro ballers are taller than the average Joe or Jane. Even though there are small players who thrive in the pros, they are rare.

But height's not the only important measurement for pro basketball. For those who do make it to the (W)NBA, the measurements never stop. Each and every game, every shot pros take, every assist, steal, and block they make, and every rebound they pull down is recorded. Then number crunchers crunch these numbers, or statistics, to measure players' performance. Get the inside track on basketball's game of numbers.

Reach for the Stars ➤

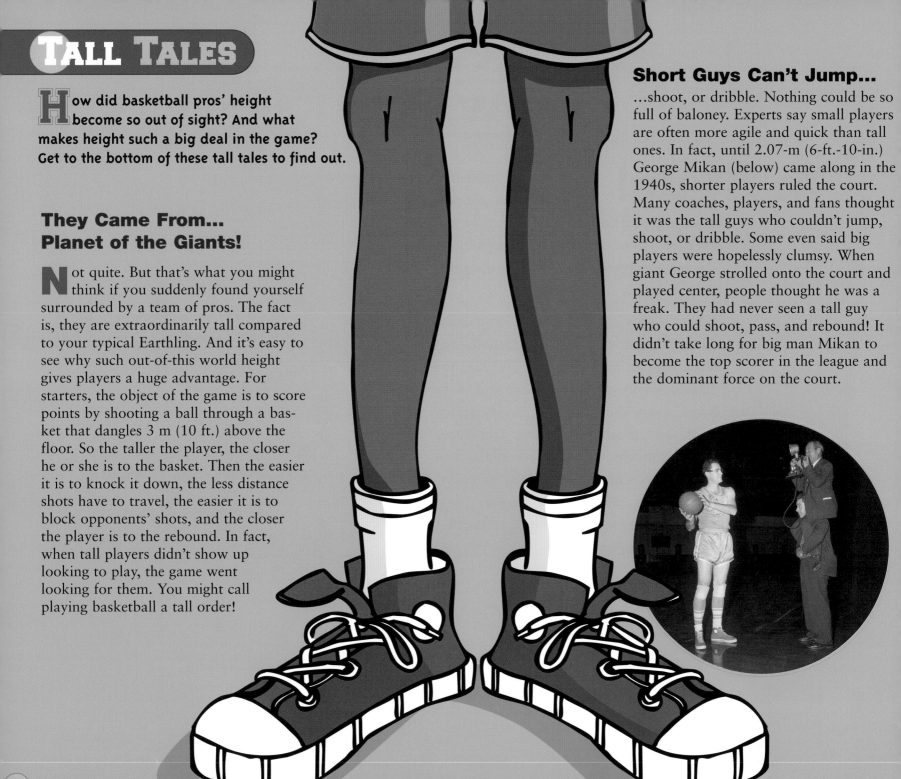

TALL TALES

How did basketball pros' height become so out of sight? And what makes height such a big deal in the game? Get to the bottom of these tall tales to find out.

They Came From... Planet of the Giants!

Not quite. But that's what you might think if you suddenly found yourself surrounded by a team of pros. The fact is, they are extraordinarily tall compared to your typical Earthling. And it's easy to see why such out-of-this world height gives players a huge advantage. For starters, the object of the game is to score points by shooting a ball through a basket that dangles 3 m (10 ft.) above the floor. So the taller the player, the closer he or she is to the basket. Then the easier it is to knock it down, the less distance shots have to travel, the easier it is to block opponents' shots, and the closer the player is to the rebound. In fact, when tall players didn't show up looking to play, the game went looking for them. You might call playing basketball a tall order!

Short Guys Can't Jump...

...shoot, or dribble. Nothing could be so full of baloney. Experts say small players are often more agile and quick than tall ones. In fact, until 2.07-m (6-ft.-10-in.) George Mikan (below) came along in the 1940s, shorter players ruled the court. Many coaches, players, and fans thought it was the tall guys who couldn't jump, shoot, or dribble. Some even said big players were hopelessly clumsy. When giant George strolled onto the court and played center, people thought he was a freak. They had never seen a tall guy who could shoot, pass, and rebound! It didn't take long for big man Mikan to become the top scorer in the league and the dominant force on the court.

Tall Advantages Can't Be Ruled Out

George Mikan (99) was the first skilled tall guy in the game, but it wasn't the first time tall guys were a "big problem." In the 1930s, tall guys usually won the rock off the center jump. So basketball's rulemakers tried to rule out their advantage. They eliminated the center jump after field goals and free throws. And to stop big guys from parking themselves under the basket and swishing shots galore, they limited the time offensive players could hang out in the paint to three seconds. And in 1952, when George Mikan virtually owned the free throw lane, they doubled the width of it to try to open it up to smaller players. But no matter what new rules they made, George just adjusted his game. Eventually, many teams concluded the only way to beat Mikan was to play tall guys who had equal skills or better. And that's how tall players rose up to rule the pro game.

Jumping Makes Players Taller

You bet it does! When players jump up, they instantly gain height. As they run up to a jump, bend their knees, and swing their arms up, they push down on the ground. Then, because there is an equal and opposite reaction for every action in our universe, the ground pushes back up, launching them into the air. Some pros rise, or vertically leap, 0.9 to 1.1 m (3 to 3 1/2 ft.) off the floor. So if they're 1.96 m (6 ft. 5 in.) tall or more, they can reach about 3 m (10 ft.)—the same height as the basket. And even though that extra height lasts only for a moment, it not only brings them closer to the basket, it can also give them a chance to take a clear shot over an opponent's head, block a shot, or deliver a monster jam. Slam-dunk!

★ STAR ★

Muggsy Bogues, basketball's smallest pro at 1.6 m (5 ft. 3 in.), always used his size to advantage. Even as a kid, the awesome point guard could sneak up on opponents and quickly steal the ball like a mugger. So his friends called him Muggsy and the name stuck.

Muggsy Bogues

TIP

Up against a taller, bigger defender? Don't panic. If you're smaller, chances are you're quicker, too. Try to get big guys or gals moving, so you can beat them. Fake one way then go the other way past the big hooper.

When Tracy McGrady got his hands on the ball in 2002–03, he seemed to do no wrong. The ball-slinging shooter fired and jammed the ball through the hoop all season long. Tracy won the NBA scoring championship with a remarkable 32.1 points per game. Check out Tracy's season stats and get the inside scoop on the numbers that measure basketball players' performance.

G	MPG	FGM–A	FG%	3PM–A	3P%	FTM–A	FT%	RPG	APG	SPG	BPG
75	39.4	829–1813	.457	173–448	.386	576–726	.793	6.5	5.5	1.65	.79

G Games played

MPG Minutes per game

The number of minutes Tracy plays each game is collected over the entire season. Then the average, or typical number of, minutes he played each game is calculated. Tracy logged lots of minutes this season.

FGM–A Field goals made–attempted

FG% Field goal percentage

Every time Tracy makes a basket within the painted semicircle around the hoop, he's credited with a field goal worth two points. Basketball's number crunchers divide the number of field goals attempted by the number made to find this stat. Top pro shooters have field goal percentages, over .500. That means they sink a bit more than half their shots. But remember this: they're shooting under game conditions. In practice, players can knock down close to three-quarters of their shots.

3PM–A Three-point shots made–attempted

3P% Three-point shot percentage

Players shoot three-point shots from outside the three-point line—7.3 m (23 ft. 9 in.) away from the basket. To calculate this stat of Tracy's, divide the number of shots attempted by the number made. Top three-point shots in the (W)NBA post numbers over .400—less than the top field goal percentages, because the farther away players get from the hoop, the harder it is to make the shot.

FTM–A Free throws made–attempted

FT% Free throw percentage

Tracy rates as a good free throw shooter. The (W)NBA's top free throw shooters post percentages of .900 or more. A percentage of .800+ marks an excellent free throw shooter, .700 to .800 a good one, .600 to .700 an OK one, and any less than that a desperately-needs-to-improve free throw shooter. This stat is found by dividing the number of free throws made by the number attempted.

RPG Rebounds per game

This stat tracks the average number of rebounds Tracy pulls down per game. Today's league leaders post RPGs of 13.0 or more. Wilt Chamberlain, a dominant center in the 1960s, holds a record-setting career RPG of 22.9.

APG Assists per game

When Tracy makes a pass to a teammate that leads directly to a basket, he receives an assist. And don't be fooled. Assists are a sign of strong playmakers—not sissies. League leaders may average nine or more assists per game.

SPG Steals per game

Tracy knows there's more than one way to steal the ball. Players can take the ball away from an opponent, intercept a pass, swat the ball to a teammate, or make an opponent hold the ball until the he's forced to hand it over. Quick-witted players who are thinking one or two moves ahead of the game often get a high number of steals.

BPG Blocks per game

Here's the average number of shots Tracy blocks per game. The taller the player, the better the shot blocker. Experts say no other stat links so closely to players' height. The fact is, leading shot blockers in the WNBA usually stand 1.96 m (6 ft. 5 in.) or taller and those in the NBA often stand more than 2.13 m (7 ft.) tall.

TO Turnovers

This stat counts the average number of times Tracy lost the ball to the other team during a game through bad dribbling or passing or committing fouls.

PF Personal fouls

Each time a player makes illegal contact with another player he gets charged with a personal foul. This stat shows the average number Tracy got per game.

PPG Points per game

Here's the most closely watched stat in pro basketball: the average number of points a player scores per game. Players score points by knocking down field goals, three-point shots, and free throws. And whoever racks up the most points per game throughout the season wins the scoring championship. In 2002–03, Tracy won hands down averaging a phenomenal 32.1 points per game. That's the highest scoring average the NBA has seen since Michael Jordan scored 32.6 points per game in 1992–93.

In 1962, Wilt Chamberlain went on a scoring tear against the New York Knicks. The superstar center scored 100 points in a single game—a scoring feat no player had ever thrown down before or since.

PPG
32.1

What's a triple-double?

Players get a triple-double when they rack up double digits in three of the following five categories in the same game: points, assists, rebounds, steals, blocked shots. Experts say it's a measure of a player's all-around ability.

STAR ☆

In 2003, Lauren Jackson led WNBA scorers with a rocking average of 21.2 points per game. What's more, the high-scoring ball hound crashed the boards for an average 9.3 rebounds a game and closed out the season as the league's Most Valuable Player.

Lauren Jackson

Hot Hands:
The Cold, Hard Facts

Swish! Swish! Swish! When a player goes on a hot shooting streak, sinking one shot after another, people say he or she has got "hot hands." But according to a scientific study, hot hands don't exist. In 1985, scientist Amos Tversky studied every shot the Philadelphia '76ers took throughout the entire season. And he found that a player's chances of knocking it down just after successfully sinking a shot didn't go up at all. In fact, they remained exactly the same.

LeBron James

As Good as Advertised?

No player has ever entered the NBA with as much hype as LeBron James. In 2003, it seemed like all sportswriters, coaches, and fans could talk about was LBJ. They marveled how the phenomenal guard was just 18 years old, was the NBA's number one draft pick straight out of high school, and had inked a shoe deal worth $90 million before ever setting foot in the NBA.

And they openly wondered whether LBJ could live up to all the hype. But the rookie Cleveland Cavalier did not disappoint. By mid-season, sportwriters said he was "the best 18-year-old b-baller ever" and everybody was jabbering about his impressive points-per-game stats. Everybody except LBJ, that is.

"Individual stats don't mean a lot to me," he said. "I feel I get my teammates into the game and they'll always be there for me." NBA coaches agreed. They said LeBron scored as needed, put the team first, and was usually thinking a few moves ahead of the action. LeBron won the Rookie of the Year award. He closed out the season with an amazing 20.9 points per game average! He joined legendary superstars Oscar Robertson and Michael Jordan as the only players to average more than 20 points, 5 assists, and 5 rebounds per game in their rookie season. Talk about measuring pros by numbers!

OFFENSE vs. DEFENSE

Whap! Your teammate jumps up and deflects the opening jump ball to another teammate—and suddenly you're on offense. Seconds later, you score. Da-dunk! So the opposition automatically gets the ball and instantly you're on defense.

Apart from a few heart-thumping scrambles when the ball is loose and up for grabs, your team either has the ball or doesn't. You're either on offense—trying to create open shots to score—or defense—preventing your opponents from taking open shots. And you must be ready to switch from one mode to the other at the drop of a hat, er, ball.

What's more, no matter how well any one player can shake and bake past the opposition, your team must work together to be effective. Discover how teamwork is the key to great offensive and defensive moves. And find out the secrets behind the shooter's touch.

Take Aim and D Up! ➤

Ready for some action? Get set to give-and-go and pick-and-roll just like the pros. Check out some of basketball's basic offensive and defensive moves.

Give-and-Go

You're on Offense

Player **A** has the ball just outside the paint and a defender, Player **C**, in front of him (1). **A** passes the ball to a teammate, Player **B**, then cuts straight for the basket, catching his defender, **C**, off guard (2). **A** is open and **B** fires him a quick bounce pass (3) for an uncontested layup or dunk (4). Sweet!

You're on Defense

Player **C** is guarding **A**, who has the ball just outside the paint (1). **A** passes the ball to his teammate, **B** (2). If **C** relaxes now, as it's natural for many defenders to do because their defensive assignment no longer has the ball, chances are **C** will get burned. In fact, that's precisely why the give-and-go is so effective. Once an opponent no longer has the ball, defenders usually ease up and then their opponents can beeline to the hoop unguarded. So **C** shouldn't relax. **C** should maneuver to stay between **A** and the ball.

Stars in Action

Play Your Position, Dude!

When teams go to battle, they send five players each onto the court. Even though any player can play anywhere, centers usually go to work closest to the basket, guards farthest away, and forwards somewhere in between. Here's the skinny on each position:

Point Guard
• Jason Kidd
• Teresa Weatherspoon

Don't be fooled by a point guard's size. Though point guards are often the team's shortest player, they do a huge job. They run the team's offense. Point guards bring the ball up and down the court, take it to the hoop, fire off passes, call out plays, and, yes, even bury the ball. Point guards try to break up the opposition's defense and feed the ball to their teammates. They often work at the top of the key, or point, and have their hands on the ball more than any other player. No wonder they're usually the best dribbler and passer on the team!

Shooting Guard
• Allen Iverson
• Cynthia Cooper

The name of this position makes no bones about it. The job of a shooting guard is to shoot on target, especially at crunch time when games are on the line. Shooting guards are usually taller than point guards, good ball handlers, and deadly three-point shooters. They set and work off screens then take off to get open to shoot. On defense, they try to force the opposition to turn over the ball, steal the ball, and shutdown the opposition's offense.

Pick-and-Roll

You're on Offense

Player **A** has the ball. She can't shoot, or pass, or shake her defender, **C**, loose (1). She calls for a teammate to set a pick, or screen, to shield her from the defender so she can make her move. **A**'s teammate, **B**, steps in so her chest faces **C**'s shoulder. **B** plants her feet wide apart, holds her hands and arms close to her body, and stands still like a roadblock (2). This stops the defender from getting around her, and frees **A** up. Then **A** hotfoots it past the defender and **B** rolls, or pivots, opening herself up to the ball (3). Now **A** can take it to the hoop for the shot or pass the ball to **B** to shoot (4).

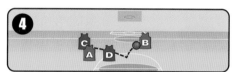

You're on Defense

Player **C** is guarding the ball handler, **A**, making it impossible for her to shoot or pass (1). Suddenly, a pick, **B**, steps in to screen the ballhandler (2). What does **C** do now? Try to "fight" past the screen by stepping out her front leg and hurling her arm and shoulder forward to move past the screen. If **C** can't get through, she calls "switch" to let her teammates know to change defensive assignments—a.k.a. players. That way her teammate, **D**, who was guarding the screen, **B**, can move out to challenge the ball handler, **A**, and **C** can cover **B** by keeping her body between **B** and the ball.

Small Forward
- **Vince Carter**
- **Chamique Holdsclaw**

Who ever said small forwards are small? Pro women usually stand 1.8 m (5 ft. 11 in.) to 1.9 m (6 ft. 3 in.) tall, and pro men tower 1.93 m (6 ft. 4 in.) or more. Small forwards are often a team's most versatile player. They shoot from the post—just out-side the lane—take it to the hoop for close-up layups and dunks, and crash the boards for rebounds. On defense, small forwards block shots and roadblock drives to the basket.

Power Forward
- **Kevin Garnett**
- **Yolanda Griffith**

Power forwards stand tall—a little shorter than a team's center but taller than the small forward—and often carry lots of bulk, er, muscle. They're monsters on the boards. No joke! It's their job to crash the boards at both ends of the court to pull down rebounds and shoot or pass. That way they can grab second-scoring chances for the team and rob sec-ond-scoring chances away from the opposition. Power forwards also throw their weight around on defense, blocking shots with a single swat.

Center
- **Shaquille O'Neal**
- **Lisa Leslie**

Centers are usually the tallest player on the team and they use their height and size to advantage. On defense, they'll park near the paint and move in to cut off drives to the basket, block shots, and pull down rebounds. On offense, they'll stand near the basket to shoot over opponents' heads, pass to open teammates, and deliver monster jams. Slam-dunk!

THE SHOOTER'S TOUCH

B-b-bing! A shot hits the rim and...drops in! Yesss! The fans roar and the shooter soars. Some say it's just a lucky bounce. But others say it's the shooter's touch. Just what do they mean? Is the shooter's touch a real thing? You bet! Get the inside scoop on the science of shots that drop.

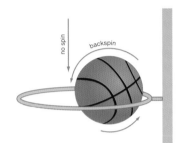

Drop In with Spin

A handful of backspin helps the rock drop down. No joke! Top scorers put backspin on the ball. Backspin makes the ball spin like a top. The ball spins backwards in a direction toward the shooter as it flies through the air to the hoop. And if the ball hits the rim or backboard, backspin can help knock it down. Here's how. When a shot without any spin strikes the rim or backboard, it bounces off at the same angle and height it bounces in at. But when a shot has backspin, it pulls back and bounces down as it hits the rim or backboard, making it more likely to drop through the hoop. Ta-dah!

Not What It Seams?

Just how do b-ball's gunslingers put backspin on the ball? It's not by doing anything fancy. It all starts by getting a good grip on the ball. Shooters hold the ball so its seams run across their hand rather than down. They use their fingers—not the palm—to grip the ball along a seam. This helps them control the path of the shot. Then they release the ball by rolling it off their fingers, which makes the ball spin backward. Shooters follow through with a wrist flick that adds even more backspin. It's enough to spin your head around!

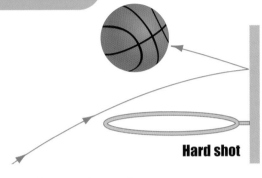

Hard shot

A Soft Touch

Ever heard people say top scorers have a "soft touch?" Top scorers know that when soft shots hit the rim or backboard, they rebound closer to the hoop than hard shots—and often bounce right in. That's because soft shots bounce with less kinetic, or moving, energy than hard shots. So great shooters try to put the ball on target with as little force as possible. They shoot the ball up and out in an arc, so it's likely to drop through the hoop on its way back down—sometimes with a little help from their friends, a.k.a. the rim and backboard.

Soft shot

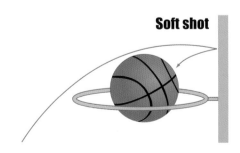

An Impossible Shot to Block?

During the 1970s and 80s, Kareem Abdul-Jabbar had a skyhook that was unbeatable. Experts say it's the greatest offensive weapon in basketball history. When the 2.18-m (7-ft.-2-in.) center unleashed it, he jumped up with the ball raised in his hand and swung it right over defenders' heads into the hoop. Kareem let his skyhook go from so high up that no one could block it!

Defense = Hard Work

Unlike scoring, which requires skill and nets players glory, defense is plain, old hard work. That means anybody who has the desire to play defense can do it, and do it well. Even though there aren't nearly as many stats to measure a player's defensive performance as there are for offense, playing defense isn't any less important. In fact, experts say great defense wins championships.

TRY THIS!

How can you make yourself taller to shoot? Jump up like the pros! How much taller can you make yourself? Try this experiment and see.

YOU WILL NEED

- outdoor wall you can mark with chalk
- chalk
- chair
- tape measure
- friend

1 Stand at the wall. Have your friend mark with chalk where the top of your head hits the wall.

2 To measure your height, hold one end of the tape measure at the ground while your friend stands on the chair and reads the tape measure at the chalk mark. Measure all chalk marks this way.

3 Stand and extend one arm as high as you can. Your friend marks the top of your hand with chalk. How much taller are you?

4 Stand at the wall with the chalk. Jump up with one hand up and mark the wall with the chalk as high as you can.

5 Repeat step 4 but this time bend your knees to jump. What happens if you bend your knees more? Less?

6 Repeat step 4 but this time bend your knees and swing your arms up just before you take off.

How high can you go? How much taller does this make you? (Check your results on page 64.)

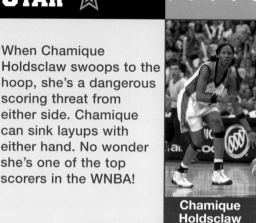

STAR ★

When Chamique Holdsclaw swoops to the hoop, she's a dangerous scoring threat from either side. Chamique can sink layups with either hand. No wonder she's one of the top scorers in the WNBA!

Chamique Holdsclaw

You're in a one-on-one situation in the post—to one side of the free throw lane. You've got the ball. A giant defender stands between you and the basket, breathing hot air down into your hair. Or you're the defender. You're the only thing that stands between the basket and a shooter with a hot pair of hands. What do you do? Be prepared to face your opponent.

The Defender

Know Your Opponent

Does your opponent dribble with her right hand or left? Does she like to go to the right or left? Move half a step toward that side to force her to go the other way. That way she has to maneuver on the side she's less comfortable on. What are her favorite spots to shoot from? Deny her those spots. Edge her into other areas on the court, where she may shoot less confidently and accurately.

Make Yourself Bigger

But not by standing tall. Stay low in the triple-threat position (see page 44), so you can move any which way once your opponent makes a move. Then hold your arms and elbows out to the side to take up more space. That way you create a bigger roadblock, making it harder for your opponent to get around you. But if she manages to slip by you anyway, jump back to reposition yourself between her and the basket. Make it your mission to stay between her and the hoop.

Watch Your Opponent's Bellybutton

It may sound wacky, but it works. When your opponent first gets the ball, she's at her most dangerous, because she can dribble, pass, or shoot. And whichever move she makes, she'll likely try to fake you out, so you go one way and she can go the other. Players can fake with the head, shoulders, hands, feet, or ball. But they can't actually move anywhere without their bellybutton. So wherever the bellybutton goes, your opponent's sure to follow!

Anticipate the Move

Your opponent is one step ahead of you. She knows what she's going to do and you don't. So your opponent can act before you can react. In order to cut down this advantage, try to anticipate what she's going to do. What does she usually like to do in these situations, for example? Pass? Shoot? That way, you're already one step toward cutting off her drive to the basket, blocking her passing lanes, making sure she has no room to shoot, or waving a distracting hand in the line of her shot.

Grab the Rebound

If your opponent gets a shot away, assume it will miss and pound the boards for the rebound. That way you deny your opponents a second chance to score. What's more, you nab a chance for your team to take it to the hoop and knock it down. As soon as the shot heads to the rim, box out your opponent. Turn to face the basket and keep your body between her and the basket. Make contact with her so you can move with her. As the ball bounces off the backboard or hoop, leap up to grab it with both hands. Whap!

The Shooting Threat

Know Your Opponent

Is your opponent a defensive demon? Does he like to block shots? Will he guard you aggressively, trying to force you to go where you don't want to go? If so, are you faster than him on your feet? Can you blow past him and beat him to the hoop? If so, can you spur him off balance with a few pump fakes over your head? Or can you move your feet first one way then the other, so he starts moving one way and you can go the other?

Be Unpredictable

You have the edge. You have the ball and you know what you're going to do. Your opponent doesn't. You can act before he can react. So try to play this advantage for all it's worth by making a move the defender doesn't expect. Vary your routine. Get comfortable using a variety of dribbles and fakes. Learn how to shoot from different spots both inside and outside the lane. And practice shooting with both hands. That way you'll be a shooting threat that defenders can't predict how to shut down.

Be a Team Player

When you're on offense, you want to create open shots for yourself or your teammates. If you've got the ball and you're closely guarded by a defender, there are two things you can do. You can shake him loose with a combination of dribbles and fakes to get open to shoot. Or you can pass the ball to an open teammate to take the shot. Always remember: when a shot goes in the basket, the whole team scores no matter who knocks it down.

Grab the Rebound

Think like a great shooter: expect your shot to drop, hitting nothing but net. Swish! Nevertheless, once your shot is rimbound, follow it for any rebound. Think of it as a second chance to score—and keeping the ball out of your opponents' hands. What's more, as the shooter, you have the best view of the shot and best idea where it'll end up. Head to the spot under the hoop where you think the ball will fall. Jump up and grab it with both hands. Then leap right back up for another shot. Whoosh!

Offense and Defense Off the Ball

Players spend lots of time playing defense and offense off the ball. Here's how to be "on the ball," when you're off the ball.

Offense

Keep your eye on the ball. Move into the post—the area on either side of the paint—and try to get open for a pass. Step toward the defender who is guarding you. Pivot and turn so your back is toward the defender and you're facing the player with the ball. Maintain body contact with the defender to keep him behind you. Have your hands up ready to receive a pass.

Defense

Don't relax if the opponent you're guarding doesn't have the ball. Keep yourself between your opponent and the ball. Watch the ball and your opponent at the same time. Use touch or body contact to tell where your opponent is rather than looking at her. Keep a hand up or take a half-step into the passing lane between your opponent and the player with the ball to prevent your opponent from receiving a pass, or even to intercept the ball.

What's the difference between man-to-man and zone defense?

In man-to-man defense, each player guards a specific player on the other team. In zone defense, each player guards a specific area of the court and any player who enters that area. If you can play man-to-man, then you can play zone. That's because you'll know how to guard a player once he enters your zone.

**Bill Russell
Wilt Chamberlain**

When Mr. Defense Met the Ultimate Scoring Machine

The year was 1959 and Mr. Defense, a.k.a. Bill Russell, and the Ultimate Scoring Machine, a.k.a. Wilt Chamberlain, were going head-to-head for the first time.

The game was billed the battle between "the unstoppable offensive force and the immovable defensive object," and it was sold-out. They were both giant centers, and they both dominated the court like no other. While Bill shut the opposition's offense out of the lane, Wilt went on scoring rampages that tore up the opposition's defense and left the NBA record book in shreds.

When Wilt's feet left the floor for his first jump shot of the game, Bill was right there with him to block the shot. Wham! The two went at it all night. While Bill succeeded in foiling Wilt on several shots, Wilt succeeded in sinking a good 30-points worth. And so began one of the most intense rivalries basketball has ever seen. Over the next ten years, Mr. Defense and the Ultimate Scoring Machine met 142 times. They inspired each other to play at the very top of their game, showing once and for all that it takes both defense and offense to make exciting basketball.

THE COURT

An official NBA court is 29 m (94 ft.) long.

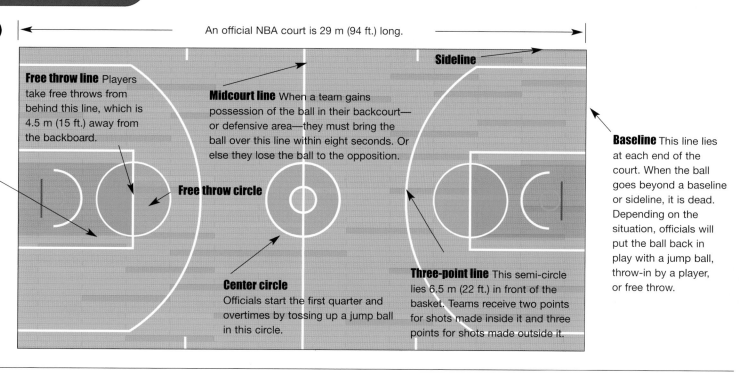

Free throw lane Also called the paint, key, or foul lane, this is the best area for shooting. Offensive players cannot stand in this area for more than three seconds without shooting. While defensive players cannot be there for more than three seconds without closely guarding an offensive player.

Free throw line Players take free throws from behind this line, which is 4.5 m (15 ft.) away from the backboard.

Midcourt line When a team gains possession of the ball in their backcourt—or defensive area—they must bring the ball over this line within eight seconds. Or else they lose the ball to the opposition.

Sideline

Free throw circle

Center circle Officials start the first quarter and overtimes by tossing up a jump ball in this circle.

Three-point line This semi-circle lies 6.5 m (22 ft.) in front of the basket. Teams receive two points for shots made inside it and three points for shots made outside it.

Baseline This line lies at each end of the court. When the ball goes beyond a baseline or sideline, it is dead. Depending on the situation, officials will put the ball back in play with a jump ball, throw-in by a player, or free throw.

THE PLAYERS

Each team plays with five players on the court who play the following positions:

- The point guard is the team's playmaker who brings the ball up and down the court to set up scoring chances.
- The shooting guard tries to get open to shoot, shut down the opposition's offense, and steal the ball.

- The small forward shoots from the post, dunks the ball, pulls down rebounds, blocks shots, and stops drives to the basket
- The power forward crashes the boards at each end for rebounds, and blocks shots.

- The center is usually the team's tallest player. Centers use their size to block shots, pull down rebounds, shoot over opponents' heads, and slam monster jams.

HOW TO PLAY

- The object of the game is to score points by putting the ball through the basket. Teams receive one point for successful free throws, two points for shots made inside the three-point line, and three points for shots made outside the three-point line. The team with the most points wins.

- An NBA game has two 24-minute halves with a 15-minute intermission between halves. Each half is divided into two periods of play 12 minutes long with a two-minute break in between.
- When a team has the ball, it is on offense.
- When a team is without the ball, it is on defense.

- Once one team scores, the opposing team automatically gets possession of the ball.
- Once an NBA team gets possession of the ball, it must attempt to shoot within 24 seconds or else give the ball to the opposition. Likewise, a WNBA team must attempt to shoot within 30 seconds.

- A game cannot end in a tie. If the score is tied at the end of the fourth quarter, five-minute periods of overtime are played until one team has more points at the end of an overtime period.

Air ball — a missed shot that doesn't touch the basket or backboard

Alley-oop — when a player catches a pass while jumping in midair and dunks it to score

Assist — a teammate's pass that leads directly to a field goal

Backboard — flat, see-through rectangle attached behind the rim of the basket

Backcourt — the half of the court where a team plays defense

Backdoor — when one player passes to a teammate and, as the defenders follow the ball, another player from the opposite side of the court cuts toward the basket to catch a pass for an open shot

Bank shot — a shot aimed at the backboard so it "banks," or deflects, into the basket

Baseball pass — a long, overhead pass thrown like a baseball catcher

Basket — the rim and net the ball drops through to score; also, a field goal or score

Behind-the-back — a skillful dribble or pass made from behind the back often without looking

Bounce pass — a pass bounced on the ground to get past a defender

Box out — putting your body between the basket and an opponent to block the player from getting a rebound

Brick — a heavy shot without the shooter's touch

Bury — sink a shot right in the basket

Cager — a basketball player

Channels — the black lines between the panels on a basketball that help players grip the ball

Chest pass — when a player snaps the ball from his chest to a teammate's chest

Crash the boards — go after rebounds aggressively

Cut — a fast move usually toward the basket to get in position to shoot

Defense — preventing the opposition from scoring

Deny the ball — a play or move to prevent an opponent from getting the ball

Dish — a pass or passing the ball

Dribble — bouncing the ball while controlling it

Drive to the basket — moving quickly toward the basket with the ball

Dunk — scoring by jumping up and pushing the ball down through the hoop with one or both hands; also called a slam dunk or jam

Fake — trying to deceive your opponent by moving your body or the ball one way then going the opposite way

Fast break — quickly moving the ball down the court to try to get ahead of the opposition's defenders and score

Feed — pass to a teammate who is in position to score

Field goal — a basket worth two or three points

Field goal percentage — number of field goals attempted divided by number of field goals made

Foul — illegal contact with an opponent that is penalized by giving up the ball to the opposition or having the fouled player take one or two foul shots, or free throws

Free throw — an unguarded shot worth one point taken from behind the free throw line; players get free throws when they are fouled, so free throws are also called foul shots

Free throw percentage — number of free throws attempted divided by number of free throws made

Frontcourt — the half of the court where a team plays offense, trying to score on the basket

Give-and-go — an offensive play in which a player passes to a teammate then cuts toward the hoop for a return pass to score

Goaltending — when a defender illegally interferes with or touches the ball while it is on, over, or above the rim

Hang time — the amount of time players can hang in the air to shoot

Hoop — basket or rim; also slang for playing basketball

Hook shot — a high arcing, or sweeping, shot that is tough to block

Hot hand — a player who scores a lot and seems to have the shooter's touch

In the paint — in the free throw lane—the painted area of the court in front of the basket

Jump ball — when an official tosses the ball between opposing players who try to hit it to their teammates

Jump shot — when a player jumps up to release a shot

Key — the area of the free throw lane and free throw circle

Kicks — slang for sneakers

Knock it down — to score, sinking the ball through the basket

Layup — a shot made by leaping up under the basket and shooting the ball with one hand, usually off the backboard

Man-to-man — a defensive strategy in which each player guards a specific player of the opposition

Micropump — a small pump inside a basketball that can add or release air

No-look pass — passing to a teammate without looking in the direction of the pass

Nothing but net — when a shot goes through the basket without touching the rim

Offense — playing with the ball to score

Open man — an unguarded player

Overhead pass — passing the ball over defenders' heads

Pick — when an offensive player plants his body close to a defensive player to block the defensive player's path; also called a screen

Pick-and-roll — when a player sets a pick for a teammate then rolls, or pivots, around the defender to the basket for a pass

Pivot — keeping one foot on the floor while the other foot steps or spins in any direction

Post — the area on either side of the free throw lane where offensive players often position themselves. The low post is near the basket and the high post is near the free throw circle.

Rebound — when a missed shot bounces off the rim or backboard; also, the act of catching the rebound

Rim — the metal hoop of the basket

Rock — slang for the ball

Screen — see pick

Shake and bake — lose a defender by making awesome moves

Shoot hoops — playing or practice shooting, often in a pick-up game or playground

Shot block— jumping up to block a shot with one or two hands

Shot clock —the clock that counts down from 24 to zero seconds once a team receives the ball; if the clock runs out before the team takes a shot, they lose the ball

Skyhook — a hook shot released when the shooter's hand is at the top of the arc

Standing reach — the height players reach with their arms extended above their heads

Steal — take the ball away from the opposition off the dribble or by intercepting a pass

Swingman — a player who can play more than one position, such as shooting guard and small forward

Switch — when teammates quickly trade defensive assignments during play

Three-point shot — a basket scored from behind the three-point line, which is awarded three points

Triple-double — when a player gets double digits in three of the following statistics categories—points, assists, rebounds, steals, blocked shots—in one game

Triple threat stance, or position — a position in which a player can shoot, pass, or dribble

Turnover — losing the ball to the opposition on an errant pass, dribble, foul, or out of bounds

Vertical leap — the height players reach when they jump

Visualization — when players mentally rehearse plays by imagining themselves successfully making the moves over and over

Zone — a defensive strategy in which players guard areas of the court rather than specific players

INDEX

Abdul-Jabbar, Kareem, 57
Activities 13, 42, 57
American Basketball
    Association (ABA), 11

Ball, the, 8–11
    micropump, 10, 11
    official WNBA ball, 11
Biasone, Danny, 19, 22
Bird, Larry, 37
Bol, Manute, 45
Boston Celtics, 9, 14, 19, 20,
    27, 37
Bogues, Muggsy, 49

Carter, Vince, 29, 55
Chamberlain, Wilt, 50, 51, 60
Chicago Bulls, 20, 25, 38
Cooper, Cynthia, 54
Court, the, 16–20
Cousy, Bob, 14

Detroit Pistons, 20

Erving, Julius, 13, 46

Fulks, Joe, 41

Garnett, Kevin, 55
Give-and-Go, 54
Griffith, Yolanda, 55

Harlem Globetrotters, 21
Height, 48–49
Holdsclaw, Chamique, 35,
    55, 57

Iverson, Allen, 54

Jackson, Lauren, 51
James, LeBron, 52
Johnson, "Magic," Earvin, 42
Jordan, Michael, 25, 38, 50
Jump shot, 40–41

Kidd, Jason, 54

Leslie, Lisa, 55

Mikan, George, 48, 49
McGrady, Tracy, 50, 51

Naismith, James, 6, 8, 10, 18
National Basketball
    Association (NBA), 8, 10,
    19, 50, 52
Nelson, Don, 9
Nutrition, 33

Official basketball rules, 10
O'Neal, Shaquille, 17, 35, 55

Passing, 42–43
Peach baskets, 6, 18
Pick-and-Roll, 55

Rodman, Dennis, 25
Russell, Bill, 60

Shoes, 24, 26–27, 30
    design of, 28–29
Shot block, 44–45
Shot clock, 24-second, 19, 22
Sports medicine, 34
Statistics, 50–51
Swoopes, Sheryl, 30

Thompson, Tina, 33
Training, 32–33
    mind, the, 36–37

Uniforms, 24–25

Weatherspoon, Teresa, 54
Woodard, Lynette, 21
Women's National Basketball
    Association (WNBA), 19, 30

YMCA (Springfield, MA),
    6, 18

Photo Credits

Ray Boudreau: front and back cover, 1 (title page), 5 (bottom middle), 7, 17 (top left), 21 (middle right), 23, 24, 31, 36 (left), 58, 59; 4: Icon Sports Media; 5: Robert Beck/Icon SMI; 6: courtesy of Basketball Hall of Fame; 10: courtesy of Basketball Hall of Fame; 11: property of Spalding, a division of Russell Corporation; 13: John McDonough/Icon SMI; 14: Bettmann/CORBIS/MAGMA; 15: Ray Stubblebine/Icon SMI; 16: Thad Parsons/Icon SMI; 17 (middle): Mark Goldman/Icon SMI; 17 (right): John Biever/SI/Icon SMI; 18, 19: courtesy of Basketball Hall of Fame; 20: John Gress/Icon SMI; 21: courtesy of Basketball Hall of Fame; 22: Greg Wall; 25 (top): Ray Grabowski/Icon SMI; 25 (middle): Glenbow Archives NA-2204-17; 25 (bottom): John Biever/SI/Icon; 28: courtesy of Popular Mechanics; 29 Manny Millan/SI/Icon SMI; 30: Icon Sports Media; 32: John McDonough/SI/Icon SMI; 33: John McDonough/SI/Icon SMI; 34: Bob Falcetti/Icon SMI; 37 (top right): Darrell Walker/HWMS/Icon SMI; 37 (bottom): John M. McDonough/Icon SMI; 38: Ray Grabowski/Icon SMI; 39: Manny Millan/SI/Icon SMI; 40: Tony Donaldson/Icon SMI; 41 (bottom left): Tom Hauck/Icon SMI; 41 (top right): Bettmann/CORBIS/MAGMA; 43: Robert Beck/Icon SMI; 44: Jeffrey Haderthauer/Icon SMI; 45 (left): Manny Millan/Icon SMI; 45 (right): Icon SMI; 46: Icon Sports Media; 47: Icon SMI; 48: AP/Wide World Photos; 49 (top left): Bettmann/CORBIS/MAGMA; 49 (middle): Jeff Mitchell/Reuters; 49 (right): Miguelez/Icon SMI; 51 (main): Chris Livingston/Icon SMI; 51 (right): Justin Case Conder/Icon SMI; 52: Jeff Zelevansky/Icon SMI; 53: AJ Mast/Icon SMI; 54 (Kidd): Ray Stubblebine/Icon SMI; 54 (Weatherspoon): Isaac Menashe/Icon SMI; 54 (Iverson): Icon SMI; 54 (Cooper): John McDonough/Icon SMI; 55 (Carter): Icon SMI; 55 (Holdsclaw): Isaac Menashe/Icon SMI; 55 (Garnett): Joe Robbins/Icon SMI; 55 (Griffith): Justin Case Conder/Icon SMI; 55 (O'Neal): Mark Goldman/Icon SMI; 55 (Leslie): Manny Millan/SI/Icon SMI; 57 (left): John McDonough/Icon SMI; 57 (right): Isaac Menashe/Icon SMI; 60: Bettman/CORBIS/MAGMA.

Answers

"Odd Balls, Goof Balls, and Handy Balls" page 11: Unlike the others, the Hands-On Basketball is the correct size and shape. It also proved to help kids sink shots.

"Try This" page 13: The basketball should bounce the highest, the tennis ball the next highest, and the baseball the least highest.

"Pssst, Speedy" page 42: The chest pass will reach the receiver the fastest. It slices through the air in a straight line, which is the shortest distance between the passer and receiver.

"Try This" page 57: You probably found that the combination of bending your knees and swinging your arms made you approximately 0.6 m (2 ft.) taller. Wow!